P9-CAN-513

MAN IN HIS ENVIRONMENT

IS VOLUME

34

OF THE

Twentieth Century Encyclopedia of Catholicism

UNDER SECTION

III

THE NATURE OF MAN

IT IS ALSO THE

108TH

VOLUME IN ORDER OF PUBLICATION

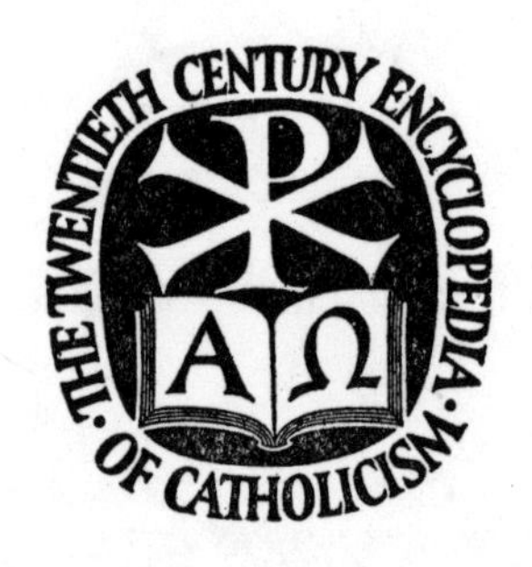

Edited by HENRI DANIEL-ROPS of the Académie Française

MAN IN HIS ENVIRONMENT

By *JOSEPH FOLLIET*

Translated from the French by MARTIN MURRAY

HAWTHORN BOOKS · PUBLISHERS · *New York*

 This book was manufactured in the United States of America and published simultaneously in Canada by McClelland & Stewart, Ltd., 25 Hollinger Road, Toronto 16. It was originally published in France under the title *L'Homme Social,* © Librairie Arthème Fayard, 1962. The Library of Congress has catalogued The Twentieth Century Encyclopedia of Catholicism under card number 58-14327. Library of Congress Catalogue Card Number for this volume: 63-17332. The Catholic University of America Library has catalogued this volume based on the Lynn-Peterson Alternative Classification for Catholic Books: BQT184.T9v.34/HM51.66. Suggested decimal classification: 572.

First Edition, September, 1963

NIHIL OBSTAT

Joannes M. T. Barton, S.T.D., L.S.S.

Censor Deputatus

IMPRIMATUR

Georgius L. Craven

Episcopus Sebastopolis, Vic. Cap.

Westmonasterii, die XXV JUNII MCMLXIII

H-9543

CONTENTS

I. What Is Society? 7
What Is Society? 8
Animal Societies 9
Human Society 10
Persons and Ends 11
Society Is a Relational Being 13
The Nature of Society 14
Person and Society 15
Does Society Corrupt? 17
Man in Society 18
Function, Status and Rank 19
Function and Authority 22
Constraint and Society 24
Is There a Social Instinct? 25
The Social Contract 28
Association and Community 29
Infra-social, Para-social and Social 31
Impersonal, Personal, Interpersonal and Social 37
Tensions 41
Forms, Structures and Institutions 44
Collective Representations 47
Behaviour and Custom 53
Mentalities and Opinion 55
Fact and Law 56
The Uniqueness of the Social Phenomenon 58
Are Social Facts Things? 60
The Social Sciences 61

II. The Direction of Social Life 64
The Genesis of Moral Conscience 68
Morality and Ethics 70

Social Scientism 72
Juridical Positivism and Political Realism 75
Moral Individualism 77
Personal Conscience and Social Life 80
The Disadvantages of Double Morality 82
Social Determinism 83
Social Determinism and Personal Liberty 89
Key Figures 91
Moral Obligation 92
Social Moralism 96
Obligations, Their Unity and Analogy 100
"Open" and "Closed" Societies 103
Commitment 105
For the Person 106
Through the Common Good 109
In Justice and Love 111
Towards Progress 114

III. CONCLUSION: BEYOND SOCIETY 116

The Divine Society 116
The Law of Incarnation 118
Spiritual and Temporal 121
A Divided World 124
The Sin of the World 126
The Social Consequences of the Redemption 128
Charity 130
The Mystical Body of the Church 134
The Christian Fraternity 135
Towards the City of God 136

SELECT BIBLIOGRAPHY 139

CHAPTER I

WHAT IS SOCIETY?

Society is a phenomenon that cannot be overlooked. Wherever man lives on the face of the earth, he lives as a member of a group. We find man living in society as far back as we can go in history, and the same conclusion emerges from research into the archaeology and folklore of proto-history and prehistory.

So compelling are these facts that they have led biologists to distinguish, if not to define, man from among other earthly creatures firstly by the unique evolution of his brain (particularly in the prefrontal zone), and secondly by his social propensity, a propensity which makes possible the communication in space and transmission in time of the knowledge he acquires—a knowledge vastly superior to that of other species. To realize this superiority it is sufficient to compare human speech—"man's glory: righteous speech"—with the cries, the songs and the gestures of animals. The latter are always subject to limitation, while the possibilities of human speech are seemingly infinite.

What strikes the observer who examines man in the context of society is the multiplicity and variety of the social organisms which he creates and into which he fits. The ethnographical surveys undertaken by the Marquis de Wavrin in the Amazon basin, Claude Lévi-Strauss' researches among the Paraguayan Indians, and Margaret Mead's anthropological studies of the cultures of Oceania, all reveal an astonishing variety of structures even within a limited area, while the works of Fr Schmidt and his school or the psychological theories of Jung operate inversely but with equal validity in establishing the constants which underlie the multiplicity of phenomena.

This complexity seems to be regulated by a law of growth. As human time unfolds, so are the forms and bonds of society multiplied as a consequence of that division of labour (taking the term in its widest sense) which Durkheim and the French school of sociology have been so right to emphasize.[1]

What is society?

What constitutes this universal fact of society, and how are we to define it? Faced with such diverse forms of society as the bees' nest, the ant-hill, the family, the trades union, the Church, the State, the Academy, the United Nations Organization, what can we find that is common to each and proper to all?

Taking the term society in its most generally accepted meaning, we may define it as a stable and organic combination of individuals, each in relation to the others and all in relation to the group, within a circumscribed unity which performs an activity shared in by each of its members. This definition is equally applicable to the ant-hill and the trades union, to the bird colony and the State. Each of these societies, within its limits, is a unity. Each is given in one way or another to a particular activity and is distinguished by the particular combination of its members, each in relation to the whole, which gives it its individuality.

This definition, which may be applied to the animal as well as to the human world, excludes all idea of finality. We do not wish to anticipate any particular solution of the philosophical problem of the finality of instincts—a problem which does not concern the sciences as such at all.

[1] Throughout this chapter, as regards definitions, I shall use the right, which an author has, in default of an established terminology, to select, to utilize and indeed to coin terms to meet his needs, providing always that every term is given a precise meaning. However, should the reader be disconcerted, I shall strive to take my terms in the meaning closest to the *sensus receptus* of specialist or current usage, and at the same time to eschew unnecessary neologisms.

Animal societies

Animal societies are regulated by instinct. Traditional fables and, more recently, J. H. Fabre's observations in the form of fiction and Maeterlinck's essays on bee and ant life are sufficient evidence of the fascination such societies have always had for man. But man must rest content with observing these societies from the outside; he can scarcely do more than describe their habits and explain them in terms of biological or psychic causes. Psychological interpretation, in the strict sense, is open to the charge of anthropomorphism. Besides, the inescapable mystery which shrouds these societies only adds to their fascination.

This is one of the reasons why all explanations of human society in terms of animal society seem to be doomed to failure. How can one explain the more familiar by means of the less familiar? All such explanations utterly fail to recognize the originality of the human species, which is biologically evident in the evolution of the human brain and psychologically in the emergence of the power of abstraction and of reflex consciousness from the reasoning faculty. Yet comparison between animal and human society is all the more useful in providing certain cross-checks and analogies.

It is instructive, for example, to observe that insect societies are both more stable and better organized than those of reputedly superior creatures. . . . The perfection of a bees' nest or an ant colony is all the more striking when set against a herd of *Cervidae*, a pack of *Canidae*, or a patriarchal and polygamous family of gorillas, but it is a perfection which in essentials at least is static and inalterable. Societies of superior animals show more initiative, more adaptability. Even in a pack of wolves, for example, in pursuit of its prey, we can see a certain spontaneous coordination of movement, as though their animal instinct was verging on that elementary and basic form of intelligence which the scholastics, happily unacquainted with the Cartesian animal-machine theory, used to call the *estimative* faculty. The leader of the pack, as photographs show, wields a control over it which goes far beyond the merely biological function performed by the "queen" of a hive.

Human society

Among social phenomena, human society is unique. Although the continuity between animal and human society is substantiated by the continuity traceable in certain animal species, among vertebrates and particularly among mammals, and indeed by man's own animal nature, to the extent that it creates his bodily needs and arouses his instincts, yet the phenomenon of man, both as an individual and in society, has an irreducible uniqueness: it combines the elements of animality in a new synthesis. Our general definition of society can only be applied in general and analogical terms to human society, which calls for its own particular definition.

Human society is a system of relations between persons or groups that keeps in view a common end considered by them to be their good.

The term "system" indicates the stable, organized, even organic character of society, together with the rational element involved in it.

The term "relations" implies an arrangement, or rather a disposal, of the elements of society, each in relation to the others and all in relation to the whole. It is these relational patterns which allow us to differentiate between societies and to class them in categories. Man instinctively senses the diversity of these patterns when he passes from one society to another. For example, within the family a man is subject to his own father, while in economic society he may be on the level above him or in political society his equal. Man observes the difference of the relations in operation between father and son, between fellow workers, between fellow citizens, and in so doing he observes the differences between the societies which determine these relations.

The distinction made between *persons* and *groups* indicates the complexity of the social phenomenon, for some societies can establish relations not only between persons but between groups of persons—like the nation, which is a "global society".

The term "person" we use advisedly, as opposed to the term "individual". The person is the human individual, a subsistent being essentially indivisible, like all individuals, but differentiated from other organic and living individuals by the specific qualities of reason and its consequence, free will. In addition to its psychological sense, which we are concerned with here, the term has a juridical sense, whereby a person, in contrast with mere material possessions, is the one and only subject of law; as well as a metaphysical and moral sense which we shall return to later.

The idea of a *common end* underlies the common purpose which is the mark of every society. The fact that this end is considered desirable by all the members of a society explains their allegiance to the groups to which they belong.

Persons and ends

Our definition makes deliberate use of the concepts of *person*, *relation* and *end*. In spite of the pseudo-scientific prejudices they arouse, we find it difficult to present the problem in other terms.

How can we, in fact, ignore the personal character of the human individual? We are not prejudicing any philosophical principles if we simply state the fact that everything happens "as if" human individuals considered themselves rational, free agents, and conducted themselves accordingly. Everything proceeds "as if" men believed that society does not deprive them of their reason or free will. This fact is daily confirmed alike by human "micro-decisions" and "macro-decisions"—employing the useful, if barbarous, expression devised by economists to distinguish between decisions taken at the primary level by the person or the small group, and the decisions imposed on larger groups by their leaders. That there are ontological realities corresponding to these ordinary common presumptions is for rational psychology or metaphysics to prove. The fact that the conduct of "rational animals" often falls short of reason and that their liberty can sometimes be limited or even destroyed by particular social conditions presents a different problem which we shall examine in its proper place. But the "isms" which deny all foundation to men's beliefs and assert an absolute determinism within the social order, are bound to prove their statements not on the scientific level (for these questions elude the reach of science) but on the philosophical level.

When the person acts, he acts with certain ends in view: persons imply purposes. Hence our definition of society involves an element of teleology which perhaps some scientists will find rather shocking. Under the influence of scientism, some have attempted to exclude from sociological methodology all recourse to teleology, and to restrict themselves to efficient causality or rather to inference of the causal type. On this reckoning, therefore, we are not to inquire into the Why of social phenomena but only into the How. This exclusivism stems from certain confusions. Firstly, there is a confusion between the natural sciences and the human sciences. Natural sciences (to take chemistry, at least, since biology cannot avoid the notion of intrinsic finality without considerable difficulty) do not need to appeal to final causality, but human sciences are entirely different from natural sciences; different in their object, which is human nature, and in the method adapted to this object. Secondly, a confusion is being made between the idea of finality and the argument from design, the former being simply a partial explanation of certain phenomena, while the latter offers a complete explanation of an ontological problem. The human sciences, like the natural sciences, are not concerned with knowledge of the Supreme End and of the subordination of particular ends to this end. Remaining within the field of observable phenomena they simply assert, once again, that everything proceeds "as if" man set himself certain objectives which he strives to attain in and through society, as the experience of centuries would seem to show. Every individual who belongs to a group, be it only an angling club, with a particular object in view, or who founds a social body, be it only a road sweepers' union, in order to attain certain definite objectives, confirms the inadequacy and absurdity of explanations which restrict themselves to efficient causality alone. Indeed so difficult is it to exclude the element of finality from social phenomena that it has a habit of reappearing in sociology in the form of unconscious value judgements. To admit that people regulate their actions in accordance with certain privileged concepts which are equivalent to ends is to reintroduce final causality. Better to admit the fact than to conceal it from oneself shamefacedly.

Society is a relational being

As a result of a particular philosophical formation, or perhaps due to a certain lack of imaginative subtlety, some sociologists have difficulty in conceiving of society as a *relational being*. They tend to regard it as a self-subsisting reality, to make it a "thing". As far as they are concerned a "relational being" is simply a pale abstraction. The fact is, they have not learnt to distinguish between the subsistent and the concrete. Beings may be concrete without necessarily being self-subsistent.

We all know from common experience what a relation is, but it is hard to conceive of and even more difficult to imagine. Of all the categories of thought it would seem to be the most tenuous and the most elusive. Yet it exists for all that, even though it is not self-subsistent, and it is of supreme importance. A painting, for example, is simply a pattern of relations of line, mass and colour; once you alter these relations you make a radical alteration of the painting, even though they exist only in and through the shapes and colours.

Again, to take a classical example, what is the difference between an army in battle order and an army in rout? Both contain the same elements: troops, companies and artillery, but the former is an instrument of intimidating force while the latter is simply a disorganized rabble. Wherein lie the differences between them, in that case? Simply in an alteration of the relations between the persons and groups of which the army is composed. The example may be trite, but it helps us to grasp the essential importance of relation in social phenomena.

The nature of society

The concept of relational being puts us in a better position to understand society and its nature. It keeps us from falling into the error of regarding society as something substantial or of adopting the myth of a collective man (which mistakes metaphor for reality). Society is a pattern of relations, and each society is distinguished by its particular relational pattern just as a fabric is distinguished by its particular design, unlike linen or silk which is made up of one single substance. Social relations do not proceed from a pre-existing society, they themselves make up that society. In the last analysis, the substance of a society is formed by actual individuals who form the basis for relations between persons. The error of making society itself something substantial can have disastrous practical consequences, resulting not in the integration of the person into society but in society's absorption of the person, in the way that Hobbes' Leviathan feeds its huge bulk on the small bodies of the citizenry. As for the term "collective man", that is simply a figure of speech; when it is mistaken for reality it is the true realities which suffer thereby—the human persons who yearn both for independence and for integration.

This error frequently derives from philosophical presuppositions, such as materialism, in the case of Hobbes, and idealist pantheism in the case of the neo-Hegelians whose doctrines underlie Fascism. The error is apparent in the logic of these ideologies, according to which the part exists only in and through the whole to which it belongs. This does not concur with sociological analysis which shows society as taking incarnate existence in already existing individuals and taking its essence from the relational system for which these individuals provide the basis. Society is a reality, but a relational reality.

Person and society

Does this mean to say that there is nothing more to society than what is contained in the individuals, or more precisely, in the sum of the individuals who compose it? This would seem to be the view of individualistic anarchists and of certain liberals. To regard society as a juxtaposition or, at best, a sum of individuals is an error directly inverse to the one last mentioned.

Such a theory is emphatically refuted by the facts. Take a child born into Melanesian civilization and remove him, with his particular heredity and his particular temperament, to London, and he will grow into a man quite different to what he would have become in his native environment. Again, take the national wealth. National wealth is not simply the sum of individual incomes at any given moment, it results from the distribution of these incomes and from the capacity for production of other resources. A nation in which rich and poor are at strife and another nation in which wealth is equitably distributed may perhaps possess equal wealth quantitatively speaking, but qualitatively there is all the difference in the world between them.

Relations, in fact, are closely connected with quality, and qualitative differences are more important in the long run than quantitative ones, since they particularize not only societies but the men who are in those societies. We may point to the way in which language can express the same thought in a hundred different ways, depending on whether it is agglutinative or monosyllabic, spoken or chanted, and in accordance also with its verbal tenses and moods.

Yet although the person is a substance and as such can sustain relations, he does not possess the gift of aseity: he exists not in isolation but in a particular situation and hence in relation to other things. Indeed he cannot exist without these relations, because it is through them that he attains self-awareness and self-fulfilment. He is continually being made and unmade and remade again by them, so that at times he may seem to be no more than a cluster, a criss-cross of relations. The relational being of society has the effect, therefore, of making the person other than he would be if, by an impossible supposition, he remained unrelated, or if, more plausibly, he were part of a different relational pattern.

"By the Ganges", says Voltaire's Zaïre, "had I been the slave of false gods and in Paris a Christian; here am I a Moslem". It need hardly be said that to be a pagan, or a Christian or a Moslem is not immaterial to a person.

Society, then, does not exist apart from persons, and persons could not completely fulfil themselves outside of, and unaided by, society.

Now we can see our way to answering the necessary question whether there is more to society than what is contained in the sum of individuals who compose it. If one wants to say that society is a substance distinct from the persons who compose it, and that from it the latter derive their existence or their essence or both, then the answer must be no. But if we mean that society affects the existence of persons not just quantitatively but in a qualitative and profound way, then the answer must be yes. For an example of the qualitative differences introduced into the life of the human individual by the social factor, we have only to point to the brilliance of high civilization or the spiritual riches of the great religions.

Mathematical language is obviously out of place here. Nevertheless, if we are to pursue the analogy contained in our original question we may say that society does not simply add up individual resources, it multiplies them. There is more power in a team of haulers, heaving to a rhythm on their rope, than the mere sum of the individual efforts within the team: their effectiveness is doubled by their discipline and rhythm. Again, while the average man's muscular power is roughly equivalent to half a horse power, industrial civilization increases this human power almost beyond measure by equipping man with "slaves of iron and steel". Individual powers of memory, though immense—a fact observable in traditional cultures—must sooner or later reach a limit, but the civilization of the written word constitutes a memory of the human race itself.

Does society corrupt?

At the time of Jean-Jacques Rousseau certain "enlightened" thinkers would have objected at this point that advantages of this kind are dearly paid for by the loss of a state of nature and the human degradation that ensues. Man is born good, but is corrupted by society: born free, he languishes in chains.

Joseph de Maistre replied by pointing to the sheep which, though a carnivorous animal, in fact eats only grass. The argument is not sufficient. It is more relevant to examine the value of the distinction between the state of nature and that of society, and to ask ourselves whether human nature, made up as it is of instincts and reason, could in fact be non-social. Rousseau's distinction is really a misapplication of the theological distinction between the state of nature and the state of grace. While society is obviously not the source of morality, it may be suggested that man's sense of morality is awakened in and through his social relations, and that man derives his very concepts of personal duty and personal rights, as well as the distinction between self and non-self, primarily from experience of society.

Must we then wholly reject the theory of Rousseau and his liberal or anarchist followers? We should make certain qualifications. Some social conditions, it is true, can degrade, corrupt or depersonalize the human person. Hegel, with his "dialectic of master and slave", each corrupted by the other, realized this, and so did his disciple Marx in his description of the relations between capitalism and the "alienated" proletariat. We have only to point to the phenomena of prostitution to see an example of mutual degradation by the sexes within a particular social context.

The old question, whether men corrupt institutions or institutions corrupt men, is not really meaningful. The experience of centuries shows that individual men succeed in corrupting even the best ordered institutions, just as faulty or badly functioning institutions manage to corrupt even the best of men. Monasteries, for instance, the very shrines of holy poverty, have often overflowed with wealth and opulence. And many pagan religions have recognized and sometimes still recognize the institution of sacred prostitution.

Man in society

The person, then, with his "situation" in society is always, actively and passively, the subject of relations. Swayed by alternate centrifugal and centripetal impulses, governed by a twofold need within his own nature for both autonomy and heteronomy, at once individual and social, the human person aspires conflictingly for similarity and distinction, like a fashionable woman who manages simultaneously to "keep up with the fashion", to be like all other women, and to be "different", to be unlike all other women. Because he is social, the person needs to attach himself to the group in order to obtain the advantages and to feel the warmth of "belonging"; this entails entering into relations of similarity to the other members of the group and carries the obligation of practising the attitude which is rather scornfully called conformism. Again because he is individual the person needs to be distinct and unique within the groups to which he belongs. To some extent this need is satisfied by membership of one particular group because it involves distinction from those who belong to other groups: hence the rivalry and snobbery between classes, nations and cultures, even between chapels, families and coteries. "There's no one like ourselves!" as they say. But this only partially satisfies the tendency, and works only in the case of the weaker characters who merely reflect their own society.

As the person becomes distinguishable by the possessions which confer a status upon him so he strives to be differentiated, within the group itself, by some special position or even by privileges or honorary titles.

The effects of the interplay between the social and the individual aspirations of the person have been successfully revealed and described by American sociologists. Here the subjective is intermingled with the objective, the psychological with the social. In other words, the situation of a person results simultaneously from the conditions in which society places him, from the position which he wants to obtain and from the position he holds in his own eyes and in the eyes of other people. Thus a person's situation in society is basically objective but is affected by his own view of himself and the view which others have of him.

Function, status and rank

The most objective of these concepts, that of *social function*, corresponds to a man's job in society, or rather to the job which society gives him, whether he is a worker, employer, civil servant or artist. It is impossible to delude oneself or to deceive others about one's social function except by lying, which provides only a temporary escape.

A man's function affects his *social rôle*. Here the subjective factor comes into its own again. The term aptly suggests the actor. Identifying himself with his function, the person plays the part which is implied or thought to be implied by the function, even going so far as to adopt a particular kind of dress which may strictly not be demanded or a particular hair-style or stance or vocabulary. Hence a person's rôle in society can turn him into a "character". It can give him a mask, in the sense Jung gives the term in his analysis of personality. The habit, admittedly, does not make the monk but it helps to make him (and, *a fortiori*, the nun); the monk, however, always makes the habit. But which makes the other, the Prussian official or his braided cap?

Social status too is derived from social function, for it depends on the value—or lack of it—attached to a particular function by the person, by other persons and by society as a whole. It is often bound up with economic status, with the method and the extent of remuneration, with the degree to which one is or is not in charge of others, and it may carry with it a juridical status which is shared by all the members of a group or social category. It is a phenomenon which is always to some extent affected by opinion. Within the class system a certain possession will set a person on a certain level and give him a certain status. In some societies opinion rates the labouring class for example, taken collectively, at the bottom of the social scale. The white-collar worker employed in commerce or industry who is paid by the month will consider himself superior to the overalled manual worker who receives a fortnightly pay packet, and in the privacy of his home the manual worker himself will confirm this assessment by putting his daughter on to be a typist and his son to be an accountant. Society marks the respective status of different social categories by the sort of possessions and distinctions it gives their members. Bathroom, house, car, telephone, university degree and O.B.E.—these are marks of distinction which correspond strictly to different degrees of social status, and it is rare to find a worker in modern British society who possesses them all at the same time. None of the official speeches about the dignity of the working man can alter this fact.

Social rank derives from social status but is affected also by personal and hereditary factors. It is the position which a person, family or small group holds in the public estimation. Even in a society which rates the agricultural worker at the bottom of the scale, a man who owns four hundred acres of good farming land or even forty acres in a vintage vineyard counts as "someone". A steelworker who becomes a trade union official rises thereby in public esteem and counts for something even in the eyes of his former bosses. An impoverished peer still retains a certain market value if he bears a famous or at least a sonorous title.

In this way *social strata* develop, marked off by juridical, psychological and moral divisions which vary according to different societies and cultures. Here the person takes up a particular position whether he likes it or not, contentedly or discontentedly. A certain minimum of social contentment would seem indispensable for his full psychological development—the feeling of being in the place divinely or naturally or historically appointed for one, and of being at home there, the feeling of being useful, of belonging, of participation, of "counting". Discontent breeds uneasiness, impatience, resentment, rebellion, and here the aggressive instinct, which Adler has made the mainspring of his psychology, comes into play with its superiority or inferiority complexes. At its extreme limit discontent leads to frustration, to the belief that one's life and actions are in vain. When such feelings pervade large areas within a society they can, as Max Scheler has shown, lead to a morality of resentment whereby the habits necessary to one's own group are seen as virtues and what is practised at the level immediately above is regarded as vice: this is the relation between bourgeois morality and upper class morality, between working class morality and bourgeois morality. Or the frustration and revolt will spark off a revolutionary conflagration bringing a change of established structures and reigning ideologies which may vary in its thoroughness but is always violent, with a consequent modification of status and rank. Or else the process of change is continuous and imperceptible: in a slow and silent revolution, the lower classes may improve their status by penetrating the higher strata of society as the representatives of the latter disappear or lose ground by relinquishing their position; in imperial Rome, for example, the decadent patrician classes were eventually replaced in this way by the sons of freedmen.

Contemporary society is witnessing a twofold development which is affecting social status. On the one hand there is a general opening-up between groups and a standardization of incomes which is bringing about a marked social fluidity, while making relative status something much less clear-cut, less absolute and less permanent. On the other hand there is a growing complexity which is propagating new classes and new milieux and so multiplying levels of social status and degrees of superiority or inferiority—together with the conflicts to which they give rise. Evidence for this is at hand in the complex machinery of the middle class, upper middle, middle middle and lower middle, and in the coexisting urban societies in America described by Lynd and others.

In all these cases of course we are using the term "social" in its widest sense. The word has two very different connotations: by it we mean either that which relates to society or else that which forms the obverse of economics and relates to questions of salary, living conditions, etc. Now social status does not stem solely from economic factors: it depends on other factors such as race, nationality, intellectual culture and religion. Imagine, for instance, the possible status in the U.S.A. of a coloured man who is a recent immigrant and a Catholic for good measure. . . . Similarly, the status of a North African in France is not simply a matter of his position in the economy and his earnings, but of his background, the colour of his skin, the way in which he speaks French, etc.

Function and authority

Social status is brought into relation with authority, either by the authority which it bestows or by the authority to which the individual becomes legally or actually subject. Authority, moreover, creates, maintains or modifies social relations. Its importance, therefore, is obvious: it is the keystone of society, whose edifice it crowns and maintains.

A study of any group, then, demands a particular attention to authority, to those who wield it and the manner of their appointment, to the ways in which it is exercised and the extent of its power. A particular form of authority corresponds to a particular kind of society. We may compare paternal authority, for instance, with the authority of a trade union secretary who is *primus inter pares*, or that of a constitutional monarch in a parliamentary monarchy with that of a dictator or prophet.

There are many forms of authority. There is the sacral authority of the high priest in a theocracy or of the consecrated king in an ancient monarchy, both representing divinity among men; the most perfect example of this was undoubtedly the Dalai Lama, priest, sovereign and wonder-worker. Then there is the institutional, functional and rational authority which prevails in rationalistic societies, statutorily connected with a political or social function. Administrative authority, which primarily bears on things and affects men only indirectly, as opposed to governing authority which is exercised on persons first and foremost and relates only indirectly to things. The authority of the counsellor, the wise man, elder, senator or sachem, always indirect since it only reaches subordinates through the intermediary of governors or administrators. Spiritual authority—taken in its widest sense whether it be that of the sorcerer, shaman, fetishist or priest. The intellectual authority of thinkers, learned men or philosophers whom the public regards as "authorities". The biological, psychological, moral and juridical authority of the father or patriarch who has "rights of authorship" over those under him. The spontaneous authority, closely linked to a communicative vitality, of animators and trainers. The authority of what Max Weber calls the "charismatic leader", the man endowed with certain external qualities who attains power by the force of his personality and sometimes by a kind of hypnotic faculty like some modern dictators—Duce, Führer, Vojd or Caudillo.

Just as every age and every civilization has a *dominant economy*, a prototype which sets the pattern for the other aspects of the economy, such as the landed estate in the case of rural civilization, the small family business in the case of liberal capitalism and big business in the case of monopolistic capitalism, so too every social and historical complex takes its pattern, directly or indirectly, from a dominant form of authority. To take Medieval Europe, there is a fine but strong connecting thread between the authority of the father in his family, that of the lord in his demesne, that of the abbot in his monastery, that of the bishop in his diocese, that of the monarch in his kingdom and even on to pope and emperor, the "two halves of God". All these forms of authority are exercised within a patriarchal and sacral context. A similar connection can be traced between parliamentary government, the registered joint-stock company, the committees which run societies and rallies, and the cooperative system, all within a liberal, democratic and rationalistic context.

Whatever its modes and forms may be, it is instructive to note that the word "authority" is derived from the Latin *augere*, to increase, for it does indeed increase the power and cohesion of society; while the word "chief" is derived from the Latin *caput*, head, thus expressing an idea not unlike the one we suggested when speaking of the keystone.

Constraint and society

Granted the importance of society, seeing that it always exercises some sort of constraint, should we regard what Dürkheim calls "coercion" as the essential mark of society? Are we to recognize the thing we call society by the presence of an element of coercion, whether juridical or psychological? We do not think that such a conclusion necessarily follows from our premises.

Coercion goes with society. Even when it lacks the force of law or the right of force, every society uses some coercion or, more precisely, some sort of pressure on its members, be it only through the wish to conform with the group and the fear of being left out, turned out, so to speak, into the darkness. But coercion is not a phenomenon restricted to society: it can also be an interpersonal affair. Many confusions, indeed, stem from the failure to distinguish between the interpersonal and the social.

Moreover, coercion must be seen within the whole social complex. Its essential significance is only grasped when we extend the term to cover the phenomena of attraction towards and devotion to a purpose, but at this point the term, though aptly chosen by reason of its very imprecision, becomes eventually meaningless. Social factors such as belonging, participation, cooperation, which are no less important than that of coercion, would appear to be at least voluntary, if not completely free. If they spring from constraint, then the constraint must be derived from some sort of natural force.

To be more precise, coercion is not an essential mark of society but a necessary consequence of it. At the risk of perpetrating a truism we may say that the essence of society consists simply in the association itself, in the existence of a system of relations between individuals, whatever may be its origin, form and effects.

Is there a social instinct?

We spoke above of a "natural force". Should we pursue this idea to the extent of asserting the existence of a social instinct which impels men irresistibly to form social groups? If we keep precisely to our terms, the answer is no.

In its strict sense the term "instinct" denotes a biopsychological force, the interior impulse of which gives animal species the ability from birth onwards to perform perfect and determined acts. Bees and ants, for instance, need no apprenticeship. A hen does not have to tell her chickens how to break the eggshell with their beaks. A sheep will tremble at its first encounter with a wolf even if it has never seen one before. A child knows how to sleep without help from its mother, though he does need her to teach him to regularize his sleep, and this shows how in man instinct is something relative. In this sense there is no such thing as a social instinct. Social man, like *Homo sapiens* and *Homo faber*, tries things out, feels his way and experiments before he achieves results, and these results are always an uncertain quantity, at the mercy of external forces or man's own instability.

From another angle, instinct may be regarded as an imperative law, an obscure force which irresistibly impels animals to accomplish certain actions. Neither the bird at mating time nor the mammal at rutting time can resist the urging of instinct. Only external circumstances—which include, notably, human volition—can place them outside this law. Taking the term in this latter sense we are more prepared to admit the existence in man of a social instinct. But the matter calls for closer examination, for we must remember that man can refuse to obey "social instinct", just as he can elude the instinct of self-preservation by means of suicide or the ascetical life, and the reproductive instinct by celibacy.

"The man who lives in solitude is either a brute beast or a god." These words Aristotle added as a corollary to his definition of man as a "political animal", which, incidentally, does not mean a man who plays at politics but a man who lives in a *polis*, a city. This admirable definition is supported by two humanly attested facts. Firstly there is the phenomenon of the "wild man" in his den, hidden in the loneliness of the forest like the "Wild Man of Aveyron" or the "Wild Woman of Ariège" or, more recently, the wolf-children of India—far removed from Kipling's Mowgli, although their pack constitutes perhaps an elemental kind of society. Secondly there is the "god" phenomenon, by which I mean the ascetic who for spiritual reasons renounces the company of his fellow men. Nearly all the great religions embody this eremitical phenomenon, closely bound up with the spiritual life. The hermit is radically different from that other phenomenon which is a feature of certain animal species like the *Pachyderms* and the *Canidae*, namely the lone, aged, male creature driven from the herd by a younger rival and made savage by solitude. The hermit freely leaves the company of his fellow men to derive spiritual strength from the solitude. The eremitical phenomenon is something beyond animality.

In man it is difficult to distinguish between that which derives from instinct and that which is rational or cultivated, even when we are dealing with as basic an impulse as the maternal instinct. Instincts stem from nature, but as Aristotle again reminds us, there is a second nature called habit, which can have very different origins.

It is safe to assert the possession by man of a *gregarious instinct*, relative to his animal nature, and a *social propensity* which is based both on instinct and reason. The former impels him towards the warmth and security of the group, makes solitude unbearable and drives him to imitate and to conform with the group. The importance of imitation has been rightly emphasized by Gabriel Tarde. Man's social propensity, on the other hand, leads him not just to join the group but to *form* groups, in other words, to construct and to organize them, always ready to make new experiments in social construction.

It is not hard to realize how powerless man is on his own. Left to himself and his littleness he is the weakest and most helpless being in the world. Even his upbringing, not to speak of his education in the larger sense, takes long years. At that point instinct and reason together impel man and woman to establish that elementary form of society we know as a family, whether monogamous or polygamous, in order to protect and bring up their children. Even the hermit takes with him into the desert the fruit of his contact with his fellow men. Robinson Crusoe on his island owed his survival, after all, to the provisions and tools he found on the ship, and for that he was indebted to society.

Thus every society takes the form of a rational system based on instinct and natural tendencies, rather as love builds up an affective structure on a foundation of elementary reflexes. Though this structure may rest on irrational foundations such as geographical or historical necessity within a civilization economically centred round a single or principal product, and though its logic may be based on irrational or even anti-rational postulates such as the intervention of animal spirits in everyday life, the transmigration of souls, the cult of the ruler as an incarnate divinity or class hatred, yet it remains essentially rational in the fullest sense of the term.

The social contract

Since reason plays such a large part in its evolution, are we to regard society as an exclusive product of reason and free will, finding expression in a social contract?

This contract theory, first devised by theologian-jurists as a legal fiction to justify authority and later adopted and distorted by Hobbes and Rousseau, dominates the social thought of the last century. Reduced to its salient features, common to all its post-Hobbesian exponents, it may be expressed as follows. Men, living originally in a state of nature, resolved to leave this state in order to obtain for themselves the advantages of living in society, and so drew up a pact, constituting the bond of society, whose terms empower the authorities to fulfil their functions. Thenceforward the will of each constitutes the will of all, the general will.

To refute this theory it is not enough to point, with the sceptics, to the absence of any reference to such a contract in historical documents. Such an objection is misplaced, for the drawing-up of the social contract takes place in the original state of nature, a state of pure individualism in which any kind of written agreement or oral tradition is inconceivable. But while it is impossible to prove the non-existence of the social contract it is equally impossible to prove its existence. Let it be seen then for what it is: a juridico-political fiction. It makes the mistake of reducing man to his specific differential, reason and free will, without taking account of external forces or, more important, of man's gregarious instinct and social tendencies such as that of giving contractual form to his social relations. As a theory it is not even hypothetically necessary; for authority finds a basis more solid than any imaginary contract simply in the need to promote the common good by concerted efforts.

Thus the social contract theory, after being complicated and watered down into a theory of a quasi-contract, to the point of becoming meaningless, has slowly lost its reputation and is today scarcely more than a chapter in the history of social thought or, at best, an expressive metaphor (as when Péguy, for example, says that extreme poverty constitutes a breach of the social contract).

In fact it is more than a fiction, it is a myth, to be seen in relation to the intellectual background of a particular period, characterized in its social relations by the pre-eminence of the contract, in philosophy by a certain extremely simplified concept of human nature and in its moral and legal ideas by a tendency to exalt the individual conscience and to regard the will as autonomous.

Association and community

We have just made a distinction between the society which is based on a contract and the natural society which is prior to any convention. This antithesis is reflected in the existing social order, as German sociologists, notably Ferdinand Tonnies, have perceived with their now classical distinction between the *association* and the *community*.

The word "association", derived, like the word "society" itself, from the Latin *socius*, a comrade or ally, denotes a form of society which we may in no pejorative sense call artificial, in so far as it is based not on any natural exigency but simply on the free will of those who establish it or give it their adherence, generally in the form of a contract. Within the limits of public order it is governed solely by the will of the contracting parties which brings it into being. An existing association may cease to exist or at least may change its character if circumstances are changed or if the contracting parties freely decide on different effects. Brought into being to fulfil certain precise needs and governed by its terms of agreement, the association only binds its members within the limits of their contract. It originates in a consensus of free decisions, and there, too, it finds its purpose. This is the case with a sports club or an association formed for economic ends. A man and a woman who have been living in association and fall to quarrelling are apt to use the significant phrase: "We aren't married".

It is quite otherwise when we turn to the *community*, a word which in its Latin and German etymologies implies the idea of unity, of *reductio ad unum*. The community is rooted in nature and in natural needs, without any agreement being necessary for its establishment. While it may involve a contract, it is not constituted by a contract, for it is not the product of law but of attraction and love. It demands of its members much more than the mere acceptance of limited responsibilities, it calls for a lifetime commitment of the whole self, body and soul. The community is marked also by special joys, the joys of community life which are derived from it. Every true community implies a common purpose which each of its members takes over and makes his own. The prototype of the community is, of course, the family, possessing deep natural roots, a creation of love, demanding of husband and wife a complete, unreserved, unqualified self-commitment, the source of unique, mysterious joys, a destiny at once traditional and forward-looking.

This distinction between association and community remains valid and useful as long as it is not so pressed as to become a dichotomy. Although the association does not take its origin directly from nature, it is a consequence of nature in so far as man has a natural tendency to the group. The law which underlies it corresponds to a natural human need, the need to create those groups necessary to the human person for the attainment of his ends. And though the community may spring from love, nevertheless it needs the force of law to defend its place among other groups and to ensure its interior structural equilibrium. It is significant that marriage, which is the basis of the family community, involves some sort of explicit or implicit contract.

The national community, for instance, cannot fulfil itself

without the support of the State which is primarily an association, juridical in character, which does not indeed exist in virtue of a contract but does imply some sort of public authority. Similarly, a business concern may not be able to become a complete community like the family or nation but it can develop into a working community through the linking of the individual and family lives of its members with the life of the work they share.

Rather than regard association and community as two completely separate social entities, it seems better to see them as two different and antithetical aspects of the one social reality. In accordance with man's own nature which is capable of love and of law, of partial and of complete commitment, every society contains an element of community and an element of association. The difference between them is not one of kind but of degree.

Infra-social, para-social and social

The distinction between association and community pervades the whole of society, for these two forms of society involve different relational systems and common activities in connection with them. These two conditions are necessary for the full realization of society, together with a minimum of rational organization. Thus while the term "social" can be used in the wide sense to denote a number of different phenomena, it should strictly be applied only to a more limited range, principally to *infra-social* and *para-social* phenomena.

Those phenomena are *infra-social* in which instinct predominates over reason, and the gregarious over the social tendency. They are on the fringe of the social in the proper sense. We have an example of this in the crowd and to a greater or lesser extent in the assembly or audience.

By *crowd* we mean the gathering in one place of a relatively large number of men who have come together either by accident or for vague and coincidental reasons. A typical example is the knot of people which collects on the scene of an accident or in front of a wall behind which "something is going on". Perhaps less typical is the crowd in a great demonstration or riot, together with the ubiquitous followers, gapers and hangers-on. Crowd psychology has been the subject of many investigations, not all of them serious. At any rate, they suggest that in the crowd personal and social control tends to break down in momentary hysteria and that crowd behaviour is dictated by instinct or imitative tendencies. The crowd has no organized structure: it can only be organized from outside, by agitators for example.

The *assembly* is a physical collection of people within a limited space and in this it is similar to the crowd, but it differs from the crowd in so far as the people gathered together are united by motives which are common to all and clear to each. So with a theatre or cinema audience, the congregation at a religious service, a public meeting or a parliamentary assembly. These examples indicate the hybrid character of the assembly, which may tend either towards the infra-social or the social: it tends to be infra-social when it lets itself be carried away by crowd psychology, or rather psychopathology, and to be social in proportion as its common purposes are clearer, deeper and firmer, and as the assembly is more organized and readier to engage in common activities. If the assembly originates from a pre-existing society, then it falls within the category of the social, in the strict sense of the term, always making allowance for the unpredictable character of the crowd, made up as it is of a large number of people.

It would be a mistake, therefore, to regard the crowd, or even the assembly as our social prototype.

The category of the *para-social* comprises incipient associative phenomena such as a gang of youths or collective phenomena such as the public or mass, the social class or milieu, which are the result of social conditions and do not necessarily involve any organization or common activity.

The *band* of children or young people—with which literary, scientific and artistic cliques, sets, coteries and even salons have something in common—is an incipient society, a grouping that is quickly formed, dissolved and re-formed, without any juridical ties, internal organization or fixed authority. It has the advantages of glamour, warmth and exclusiveness in regard to other societies, but it is unstable and fluid. The band is something as old as youth itself, if the phrase may be forgiven—Gil Buhet's book *The Honey Siege* shows it at work among a set of village children—as old as man's partiality for the small, restricted, friendly, welcoming, free gathering. Urban civilization, especially in densely populated areas, has seen a vast increase in these bands, perhaps because many children or adolescents find there an emotional satisfaction which they do not always get in the disorganized atmosphere of their homes. They are frequently connected with juvenile delinquency, for only a thin line divides the band from the *gang*, which is also unstable but rather more organized.

The *public*, which unlike the band is always of a considerable size, is made up of people whose attitude is primarily, if not exclusively, receptive and passive, their attentions being focused on a common point of interest. Such are the fans of a film star, the readers of a particular newspaper, the devotees of a radio programme known as "viewers" or "listeners", the audiences who go to hear a particular lecturer, the regular public of a writer or artist. All these are what we call a "public". The public is essentially unorganized and passive and the relations between its members are transitory and fortuitous. Hence it is para-social. Nevertheless, a particular public or one section of it may easily develop into an assembly, when for example the fans of a popular singer who only know him from the radio or recordings gather to hear him "in the flesh", or to mob him, to fall upon him so to speak as he steps from a plane at the airport. Or again, a public may develop into an association, as for example when some of its members decide to form a club, or to wear some distinctive badge. The technical progress of contemporary media such as the cinema, press, radio and television lends an increasing importance to this phenomenon, for its effects are penetrating existing social categories and classes and even societies and institutions. Some forms of the public are restricted to the mass.

The *mass* is an agglomeration, without any internal organization or precise boundaries, of individuals who are so similar and homogeneous as to appear identical. The social mass, like the physical mass, acts primarily by its force of inertia. In its present magnitude the phenomenon of the mass is something recent, the result of industrial urban civilization and of the uprooting and breaking down of barriers which comes with it, of the disappearance and decay of traditional communities and of new cultural movements and fashions. We may distinguish between the general *mass* itself, a phenomenon in which all social classes have a share, and the *specific masses* which by and large correspond to the well-known social categories, that is to say the working-class masses and the middle-class masses.

What we have called the *social category* is to be regarded as a classification operated by the intellect but based on actual reality. It is composed of individuals with an analogous, if not identical, function and status (together with the psychological consequences that follow from them) or, in a wider and simpler sense, of people whose social situation gives them common characteristics. In this last sense we may regard the physically undersized, the economically underprivileged, released convicts or large families as being different social categories. An example in the former sense would be the members of a particular profession or class. The bonds, usually of a material character, which form a particular category may in some cases go unnoticed by the members of that category, only being apparent to outside observers. It took some time, for example, for the working class to become aware of itself, and it was helped towards that self-awareness by the observations and theories of what we would call middle class intellectuals. The social category, then, is not to be confused with society, but it can serve as a foundation for societies built upon it. For instance, the working class has given rise to the Labour Party and, more important, to guilds and trade unions. The societies which are formed in this way are never coterminous with the entire category whence they originate, as soon as the latter has exceeded a certain number.

Social milieux are, to some extent, grafted on to the social categories, and sometimes they result from and reflect them. The socio-psychological concept of a milieu has a complexity and elusiveness which reflect the complicated and shifting social scene. It seems to be easier to sense the existence of a milieu than to define what it is. And it is not entirely accidental that in current French the term "milieu" is primarily applied to those shady circles of society which deal in vice, crime, money and politics. Yet the term can still be used to denote a man's familiar surroundings, the ambience in which he feels at home and at his ease, in which he can lead his life without constraint, without having to project an "image", except for the image which the milieu itself may impose on him if he comes into conflict with it. A man's milieu in this case is formed by his circle of relatives, neighbours, fellow workers, family friends, friends who belong to the same club or society or church, even the people he meets every day on the bus or in the train. The social milieu stands in the same relation to a "social animal" as the biological milieu to the biological animal: it surrounds, supports and restricts the individual, influencing him and being influenced by him. Its influence can be particularly marked in the case of those weaker characters who take on the colour of their milieu like chameleons. It is the combination of these individual milieux which eventually determines a larger social milieu. One can feel the presence of a particular milieu in the working-class districts of large cities: a journey from the West End to the East End of London, with the change of milieu it involves, could be registered by the senses of sight, hearing and smell. Specialized professions such as those of dons, school teachers, lawyers and soldiers tend to form rather closed milieux. To determine a specific even though vast, milieu we may use two criteria which are to be found in Roman law, the notions of *convivium* and *connubium*. Together they mean quite simply that the people who belong to a man's milieu are the people who are regularly invited to his family table or to whom he is prepared to grant his daughter's hand in marriage. This fact usefully reminds us that a milieu is not simply the result of economic conditions: it involves other factors such as race, nationality or culture. One and the same man can simultaneously belong to several social milieux. This is so, for example, with the businessman-farmer who is town-mouse and country-mouse by turns; with the servant in a great house who is sometimes more conservative than his master, like J. M. Barrie's *Admirable Crichton*; with the small businessman in a working-class district, or the small proprietor who works in a factory. The milieu then, without organization or structure, forms a link between the para-social and the social.

Turning to the social, in the strict sense of the term, we have already studied the concepts of association and community. Two terms remain to be elucidated, namely *group*, a frequently used word which causes many confusions, and the more technical term *global society*.

In its wide sense, which reflects its etymological derivation, the word "group" may be taken to mean any collection of people which involves a certain minimum degree of interaction, common activity and structural relationship. Differing from the society, which implies more than this bare minimum, the term may be applied to such diverse phenomena as the assembly, band, association, community and even a section of a society or community. One can also make a further, quantitative, distinction—useful, if unlovely—between "micro-groups" and "macro-groups".

The term "global society", coined by M. Georges Gurvitch, denotes that society which contains and embraces all the different societies of a certain time and place. For a long time this rôle was filled by the nation, which embraced what an historian of Catholic society, M. Martin-Saint-Léon, has aptly called the societies of the nation, sometimes known also as the intermediate bodies.

Some further precisions of detail will be useful here. We shall make little use of the term "collectivity", which we find too vague and general. Basically it denotes no more than its etymological root *colligere* would suggest, namely a number of individuals who are to some degree organized. By reason of its very vagueness it is a favourite term of the adroit debater. When it is said, for example, that the care of the aged is incumbent on the "collectivity", what collectivity is meant? And when it is advocated that the "collectivity" should take over the machinery of production we are entitled to ask the same question. In fact most people today who talk about the collectivity really mean the State, but they dare not say so nor even admit it to themselves.

Finally, there remains the theological distinction between *perfect* and *imperfect* societies. In this case "perfect" and "imperfect" have no reference to moral or spiritual values. A perfect society is one which itself possesses the means of fulfilling its functions, such as, for instance, the Church or the State. An imperfect society is one which cannot subsist by its own means nor carry out its mission without cooperation from other societies.

Impersonal, personal, interpersonal and social

These clarifications help us to get a clearer picture of the relation between person and society. We may distinguish four major spheres of life and activity: the impersonal, the personal, the interpersonal and the social. It should, however, be noted that distinction is not the same as separation, and in actual reality these various spheres merge and intersect.

The *impersonal* in society is practically identical with the infra-social, which forms the basis or the preliminary stage of the social, and with certain aspects of the para-social where, to use Thomist language, *actus hominis* supersede *actus humani*, in other words, where instinct prevails over reason and determinism supplants liberty. The crowd is impersonal, and therein lies its mystery, a mystery as fascinating and as frightening as the mystery of the animal world. The effect of the crowd is to weaken men's reason and free will: it is depersonalizing, anti-rational, stifling all sense of personal responsibility in the collective anonymity, in the physical and mental excitement of the moment—even though in certain circumstances the crowd phenomenon can be directed to higher ends. The masses, too, destroy personal originality and potential, creating instead a collective and indeterminate "man in the street", who must do what everyone else does. Left to the mercy of the crowd and the mass, the person would ultimately become a sort of puppet controlled by extrinsic determinisms, keeping no more than the freedom of unconcern. The predominance of the crowd and the mass in contemporary civilization has brought about the rapid increase of what David Riessmann calls the "other-directed" type of man, the man who models his behaviour on that of his contemporaries, unlike the "tradition-directed" man, belonging to a so-called traditional culture, who follows the lines laid down in the past, or the "inner-directed" man who directs himself according to the inner light of his own conscience. Of course these three types are no more than rough generalizations, with no claim to any real existence: every society comprises men of all three types and each individual can find traces of them all within his own personality. The person obstinately refuses to be depersonalized, precisely because as a person he strives to be different, to be autonomous. Hence inevitably a tension develops between the person and the mass, between the person and the crowd, a tension embodied in the conflicting emotions of attraction and repulsion which the person feels for the crowd, and giving rise by its own paradoxical nature to a simultaneous apathy and torment, conformism and revolt.

We come now to the *personal*, the proper sphere and native soil of the human individual capable of directing his activities to certain ends and of coordinating these ends in the pursuit of the particular end which constitutes his vocation and his fulfilment as a person. The personal factor is found at its maximum intensity in the interior life which is the source of a person's considered decisions and which involves attitudes and activities of the soul which have a profound importance for the person: withdrawal, reflection, judgement and decision. A person temporarily withdraws to his interior life as, so to speak, to an island or an oasis in the midst of society. Yet the distinction between personal and social, for all its validity, must not be mistaken for a dichotomy. The character which marks out a particular personality is the result of free will acting upon a temperament formed by hereditary factors and exterior influences. But to a great extent character is shaped by the education a person receives, and education means integration into a particular culture and incorporation into a particular group. A Chinese Confucianist will not have the same sort of character as a Russian Communist or a citizen of New York or Chicago brought up in the American way of life, nor will a German Catholic be similar in character to a southern Italian Catholic. A strong character, it is true, is a man with a mind of his own, but the reason can only set to work on what it is given, on the material of a particular culture or sub-culture. Finally, within a society a person will also have a certain social status, and this status, together with his economic, social and political functions and his superiority or inferiority complexes, also contributes to the formation of his character. Adapting the familiar Freudian terms to our own use we may distinguish within the person an *id*, temperament, subconscious, unconscious; an *ego*, or conscious and personal self, and a *super-ego* or social super-self which becomes part of the person's consciousness and is superimposed on the self and sub-self. But where personal and social combine, the person is not merely passive and receptive, nor restricted in activity to the personal sphere: he acts and makes himself felt in his immediate surroundings, within the milieu of his family, neighbourhood or profession which he tends to make an extension of himself: it is here that his micro-decisions are made. He may even make his influence felt over a much wider radius and make his mark on the structure or mentality of a society. One has only to think of the effect which great statesmen, great social reformers, prophets, thinkers, literary or artistic geniuses—those whom Baudelaire called "Beacons"—have had on their own times and on posterity. Even today millions of men govern their lives according to the precepts of Moses, Mahomet or Karl Marx—or more precisely according to their interpretation of these precepts.

The *interpersonal*, which comes within the immediate range of the person, is not to be identified with the personal, or the infra-social, or the para-social, or the social. It relates to something else, to personal relations taken by themselves, even though there may not be any strictly social bond involved. Thus it is to be found in its purest form as a partnership, where two persons unite in love or friendship. Where the relationship is between more than two persons the interpersonal element still remains but it is less perfect, less unadulterated. That is doubtless one of the reasons why the representatives of society often regard examples of this phenomenon in their ranks with a certain suspicion, sometimes ironically expressed. Society tolerates the love of a man for a woman because it cannot do otherwise, but it fears it and tries as far as possible to limit its effects. Evidence of this is to be seen in the practice of totalitarian parties and governments. Three people, however, form an incipient society. As the saying goes, *Tres faciunt capitulum*: three canons are enough to make a chapter. But while the interpersonal is not to be confused with the social, it is not by any means separate from it. Interpersonal relations must always be seen against a certain background, and that background is often provided by society. Love does not take the same shape in the age of Pericles and Aspasia as in that of Catullus and Lesbia, of Tristan and Iseult, of Don Quixote and Dulcinea, of M. and Mme Denis, of

Georges Sand and Musset: it is not the same at Boulogne-Billancourt as at Auteuil or in the land of Gaspard of the Mountains or in the farm at Mireille—for love is affected by time, place, culture and even economic conditions. Friendship will never be the same in the Christian era as it was in the age of Socrates and Alcibiades: we have come to distinguish between friendship as such and what M. Peyrefitte calls "special friendships". Finally, not only is the interpersonal affected by the social: it in turn may influence society. Some of our great men have been made by a woman's love.

As for the *social*, we have in the preceding pages discussed the term at sufficient length for us to be able to refrain from further prolonged analysis. It is not to be identified with the impersonal, personal or interpersonal, nor is it to be taken as an abstraction of these, for it presupposes and assumes them. It is more essentially true to itself when its unique (or *sui generis* as Dürkheim would say) relational structure is clearly differentiated from the personal, and consequently more stable and more organized, and from the impersonal, and therefore more structured, more rational, a collaboration between the personal and the social. For instance, the family is based upon a pre-eminently interpersonal relationship, and then love, the marriage contract, the alliance of love and law, interpersonal and social which it involves, the coming of children, their educational needs—all these elements turn the family into a society, a markedly structured society of the community type, without destroying its interpersonal relations or uniqueness.

Tensions

The preceding distinctions help us to understand how inevitable are those tensions which arise between society and the person. Every society invokes a cooperation between persons in a common activity and towards a common goal, but this cooperation always involves difficulties and consequently tensions. Perhaps it may be simply because the person is distinct from society and can only be integrated into it by a slow education in the acceptance of discipline, a discipline which is restricting and so inevitably constitutes a threat to him. Or it may be because every group can include certain maladjusted or even a-social and anti-social persons such as chronic perverts who upset its proper functioning. Or because societies can, for various reasons, function badly or become atrophied, or else, while continuing to function properly, oppress the person or give him the impression of being oppressed. These more or less normal tensions which are as much the result of ordinary contingency and human limitations as of the permanent conflict within persons and societies between the infra-human and the human, are further aggravated now and again by the inevitable disproportion between ambition and status, between the historical development of institutions and the evolution of human attitudes.

This simultaneous collaboration and tension is to be found to a maximum degree in community life. There are no greater sufferings, no more intense joys than those of the family circle. Likewise, there is nothing which can be so liberating or else so oppressive for the person as the home. It is precisely that element of self-commitment demanded by the community which brings about this intense degree of collaboration or tension, joy or suffering. Perhaps we should add to this the observation that in the community the person may find the connecting link between necessity and free will: husband and wife know that they have chosen each other in complete freedom and yet at the same time they know that they were predestined for each other from all eternity; likewise, their children feel that they could not have been born elsewhere than in their parents' home. The "bond of gold", to quote the old song, can of course become a heavy chain: the family bond is a bond of necessity, and its weight is the price to be paid for being able to follow simultaneously the command of instinct and the attraction of love.

The existence of such tensions is nowhere perhaps more marked than in the results of the controls which society finds necessary to impose on the reproductive instinct. Reproduction concerns society because it ensures its continuity in time and extension in space, but it can also be seen as a threat to society in so far as it tends to turn married couples and families in on themselves, apart from social life, and because it can be manifested in anarchical outbursts of violent passion which gravely endanger the family itself and other social institutions. Thus all societies have attempted with varying degrees of success to check the reproductive instinct and in the common interest to protect and regulate the family institution by a system of sanctions and taboos both secular and religious. To depth psychology and its study of the unconscious is due the discovery of the effects of this regulation upon personal conduct, and of the mental traumata it can lead to in the case of repression (taking that term in its technical sense, not to be confused with simple inhibition) or of failure to overcome certain complexes contracted during the obscure years of early childhood. These conflicts, in which impersonal, personal and social elements are all involved, can sometimes result in harrowing tensions.

Tension is cruel and often unbearable. A person may attempt to hide his tension from others and to conceal it from himself. This psychological dissimulation may take various forms such as projection, whereby the origin of the tension is identified with someone or something quite unconnected with the persons or societies concerned and even with a semi-imaginary object such as "the Jews", "the capitalists", "the Communists", "the Jesuits". Or, perhaps feeling uneasy about his social privilege, a man may assume that attitude, so derided by the existentialists, of having "a good conscience". Or he may justifiably try to rationalize his perhaps painful situation by persistently maintaining that it is inevitable and that after all in the worst of all possible worlds everything is for the best. Vice versa, he may transform his feeling of inferiority into one of superiority by adopting an attitude of resentment. These fantasies can alleviate tension but they cannot remove it, any more than cotton wool padding can remove the actual weight of chains.

Basically there are only two ways whereby a person may end the tensions which torment him, but both are ultimately impracticable. The first is to retire into an ivory castle, "far from the madding crowd", withdrawing from society into an exclusively personal territory. The only person who fully achieves this is the schizophrenic, in his world of dreams which resembles the Cabinets of Dr Caligari. This extreme case sufficiently indicates the impossibility of such a solution. The second course is for the person to identify himself completely with society, to live exclusively outside himself, in, by and for society. Today there are people who make a valiant effort to achieve this but ultimately it leads to the phenomenon of cyclothymia—periods of social exhilaration followed by periods of depression in the loneliness of the crowd and the mass. The "inner-directed" man is a potential schizophrenic and the "other-directed" man a potential cyclothyme. In fact, social tensions would appear to be both permanent and inevitable.

Forms, structures and institutions

A society, then, made up as it is of impersonal, personal, interpersonal and social elements and constituting a system of relations, takes concrete and definite form with a precise exterior delimitation and internal structural organization. This organic and determined quality is what distinguishes society from the para-social mass or public. This is the sign whereby the existence of a society may be recognized.

These limits which define a society may be geographical, as in the case of a nation or civilization, or else identical with the scope or object of the society, as in the case of partial societies which may even lack geographical delimitations, like UNESCO or FAO. Its interior structure may be simple or complex: simple when the grouping is one of persons only, as in the case of the family, and complex when not only persons but whole groups and an almost infinite number of sub-groups are brought together, as in a Church or nation.

The importance attributed by some German sociologists—and indeed psychologists and historians—to the concept of *form* is well known. According to this reckoning, societies are classed, catalogued and arranged in a hierarchy according to their different forms.

Here we shall take the term as meaning simply the general configuration of a society, the view one gets of it at first glance from the outside, the basic elements in its system of relations by which we can differentiate and classify it. Thus a syndicate differs in form from a corporation, and both of them differ in form from a company. Forms involve differentiation.

By *structure* we mean the internal organization of a society, in the sense that underneath flesh, skin and hair the skeleton forms the structure of a body and the skull that of a face, while the structure of a building is constituted by its walls and timber work. The concept of structure in fact implies an element of stability and construction—two terms to which it is related through an Indo-European root word. A social structure is the result of a collaboration between the needs of a particular time, place and milieu and human reason working upon these data. We shall use the term, then, to denote the stable and essential elements of a social reality, elements which serve as a basis for other less durable and less important phenomena, according as the reality in question is at least partly the result of rational construction. Such are for instance, in the State, the major administrative departments and the organization of the judiciary, etc. The different types of family organization such as the patriarchal family or the family-line, etc., may be regarded as its *forms*, while the internal organization of its authority constitutes its *structure*. These definitions show that the form of a given society may become the structure or a structural element of a superior society of which it is a part. Thus religious orders with their separate forms help to make up the structure of the Church of which they are a part.

We in modern France have seen the birth and growth of such a structure in the development of our Social Security organizations. With elements borrowed from two previous structures which it to some extent supplanted, namely the capitalist insurance society and the Friendly Society, the Social Security System made its first appearance rather diffidently between the two wars in the form of Social Insurance. After the Parodi-Laroque scheme it began as a plan and finally became one of our most important national economic-social structures, as well as an institution.

In certain cases we may make a further distinction between *substructures*, *structures* in the strict sense and *superstructures*. This distinction, however, is often intractable and it can sometimes also be artificial and misleading. Its relevance to the economy is fairly obvious. The economy of any given country comprises substructures in the form of roads, canals, railways, etc.; structures in the form of agricultural, economic and commercial concerns, and superstructures which are social organizations (in the restricted sense of the term "social") grafted on to the economy, like syndicates, corporations, etc. Or adapting Marxist terminology we may take substructures to be the techniques of production, structures as the economic organizations related to these techniques and superstructures as the social organizations connected with the economy. We do not take the latter to include cultural, political or religious realities, for these cannot, save at the risk of "pan-economism", be regarded simply as superstructures of the economy.

The idea of the *institution*, as we have remarked, is closely connected with that of the structure. Basically, the two terms envisage the same reality under different aspects. The institution is a juridically organized structure which the members of a society are aware of as an existing reality possessing legal status or, as Hauriou puts it, "an idea translated into fact and a fellowship made systematic". Answering certain needs perceived by the intellect, which it proceeds to satisfy in its initial charter and successive modifications, it is the result of a rational construction, law being the work of reason; it organizes structures by a legally sanctioned system of relations. Thus, to return to our earlier example, we have the insurance companies and friendly societies which originally started in individual initiative and then slowly became more organized as capitalist insurance expanded; the development of mutual insurance in all its forms; social insurance, and finally the social security system which is still only in its infancy. Not all structures are necessarily institutions in the juridical sense of the term (and this applies *a fortiori* to substructures) but all institutions are structures.

Both structures and institutions exist within an historical context and have, besides, an historical development of their own. They start with an idea, the idea results in a plan, and the plan is then realized by the authorities or by private enterprise. They grow in extent and organization, and their scope and effects are legally defined. If they fail to renew themselves in keeping with the times or to adapt themselves to new needs, then they die—either by the slow process of senile decay or by sudden collapse, when a revolution comes and breaks irrevocably the thread by which they hang on to reality.

Collective representations

Forms and structures, and the interaction between personal and social, psychological and social factors, give rise to *collective representations*. The term must be understood properly. It does not denote a self-subsistent reality, higher than and participated in by individuals, but quite simply the identity, similarity or analogy between the representations shared by a large number of persons or even to a varying degree by a whole group. The same applies to what Jung first called the "collective unconscious". This is not a sort of vast single ocean which pours its brimming waters into the unconscious of separate individuals but simply the unconscious and subconscious operating in common. Like society itself, the collective representation and the collective unconscious have a relational being.

To say this is not to question the existence or the importance of collective representations. Their existence is attested by psychology and by the history of ideas. Psychologists have shown, for instance, that the fact of their colonization has such an effect on the minds of colonized peoples that it becomes embodied in their dreams, and similarly that a very distinct social category, such as that of tramps, can be built round a single view of life. If all the various social ideas of a particular time and place, even contradictory ideas, give an impression of being related—and this impression will strike the reader of such works as those of M. Maxime Leroy—then the reason will be found in these collective representations. As for the existence of the collective unconscious, that is attested by the analysis of dreams among the most diverse peoples and by the comparative studies of folklore carried out by Frazer, Robert Graves, Georges Dumézil and others. Collective representations are inevitably affected by the collective unconscious if only through a particular "mythology"—and there are many different kinds of mythology, not excluding science fiction.

Collective representations include images, concepts, values and myths.

As examples of the first-mentioned we may cite the workers' image of their bosses, the capitalist image of the communist, the Englishman's image of the Frenchman and vice versa. Sometimes this image is simplified to the point of caricature, and so we get the little bearded French monsieur, dressy, conceited and too polite to be quite a gentleman, who figures in the popular English imagination, or the hook-nosed, egg-headed, almond-eyed, curly-haired Jew of anti-Semitic mythology. So, too, conceptions of love and of family life are profoundly affected by the image men form of women and by the image of themselves which women create in order to please men. Here we re-encounter the "social mask", for in collective psychology what a man seems to be is almost as important as what he is.

Collective representations may be abstract and general *concepts*, the concept of a particular class, for example, or of class itself, or even of man and human nature. These collective concepts generally become simplified and generalized by the very fact of their expansion, bearing only a remote relation to the scientific, philosophical or religious ideas in which they originated. Thus scientific positivism and materialism were turned into the "popular materialism" of the free-thinkers. Marxism gains ground by means of catch-cries and slogans. Catholicism also can father those by-products which the Germans call *Vulgar Katholizismus*. Investigation and thought, indeed, appertain essentially to the person, while the group simply takes over, adapts, popularizes and inevitably debases them. Take Flaubert's well-known characters Homais, the chemist, and Bournisien, the parish priest: in the popular mind they have been debased out of all recognition.

A systematically organized set of images and concepts constitutes an *ideology*. An ideology is not the same as a philosophical or theological system but derives from one in a particular geographical and historical situation. Marxism, liberalism, fascism and rational socialism, for example, are ideologies of this kind. An ideology often has little in common with scientific or religious truth, being mainly the result of circumstances, though it is regarded by its adherents as the embodiment of truth and justice. Yet it is not all falsehood: every ideology must incorporate some truths and some genuine aspirations towards justice. Ideological humbug may seem glaringly obvious to posterity but at the time is often difficult to perceive. Only now are we discovering, for instance, the part played by political feeling in the Donatist schism, or the nationalist element in Tudor Anglicanism or the political and economic issues underlying those seventeenth-century Scottish wars waged in the name of Puritan Calvinism which seem otherwise so incomprehensible.

Every ideology carries with it certain *values*, that is to say, fundamental and seminal concepts which serve as criteria for judging other concepts or form the inspiration of attitudes. Individual enterprise, for example, has become a middle-class value, and solidarity a working-class one. These values tend to be grouped together, to become organized and arranged in a system which is based on certain supreme values and is metaphorically called a scale or, as Nietzsche terms it, a table of values. Every epoch and every culture has its particular set of values, often personified in an ideal type of man which is looked to by others as a standard and model such as the *kalos kagathos* of Athenian society, the *honnête homme* of seventeenth-century French culture or the "gentleman" in eighteenth-century England. At the same time, together with its set of values, every group contains living individuals who are regarded as being particularly faithful to these values and who serve as a model for the rest of society, whether as standard examples notable for their perfect conformity or as ideal models who inspire admiration rather than imitation and yet personify the ideal which the group is striving to attain. So in a religious order one finds the model religious on the one hand and the saint on the other—each in his own way representing the values of the community.

Images, concepts and values can all develop into *myths*. This pregnant expression has at least three connotations. Firstly, there is the traditional myth—the legend, story or anecdote with a symbolic and interpretative import, like the Prometheus and Pandora myths, providing an irrational explanation of certain origins or situations. Freudian psychology has succeeded in grasping the human significance of these myths, rooted as they are in the depths of the unconscious, but it has sometimes abused them: to attach a mythological label to psychological phenomena is to not provide adequate causal explanation of them. Secondly, in the sense which Bergson and Sorel have given the word, it denotes a highly evocative yet indeterminate idea which is projected into the future and charged with emotive power: for early socialists it was the Great Night, for revolutionary trade unionism the General Strike, and for Hitler's Nazis the Third Reich. This kind of myth is not so important in itself as for the feelings and actions it engenders. Finally, in the sense amplified by M. Roland Barthès, the term is primarily applied to certain persons, whether imaginary like Don Quixote, or real like Brigitte Bardot, whose image has been so enlarged and inflated that they become the object of a cult.

Among the various collective representations special mention must be made of the *idea of the world* and the *view of life*. An *idea of the world* is not quite the same as a world-view, a *Weltanschauung*, but rather the popular and diffused version of it: a conception of the universe, of the earth and of man's place within the whole, based upon particular scientific theories and philosophical systems. Men's idea of the world could never be the same after Copernicus, Galileo, Descartes and Newton as it was before them. Our own idea of the world is being rapidly changed under the impact of Einstein's theory and space satellites.

The *view of life*—a term we owe to Paul Bureau—signifies the conception a man forms of himself, his destiny and happiness and of the meaning and purpose of his existence. Consequently, it presupposes judgements of value. Men will act differently according to the concept of human destiny which prevails in their particular culture, whether this destiny is seen as being in a future world after death (the view Christopher Dawson calls "other-worldliness") or as being both earthly and transcendental, as with Marxism, or in the immediate present, as with individualistic materialism, or as both in history and beyond history, in the world and beyond the world, as with Christianity of the classical and humanist age.

Collective representations are sometimes called *beliefs* to distinguish them from attitudes.

Attitudes, which are at once individual and collective, are the active manifestation of collective representations. Sometimes prevailing attitudes may directly contradict the established representations, thereby revealing concealed opinion as opposed to expressed opinion. When this dichotomy between the theory and the practice of a group becomes general one may conclude that its representations no longer serve their purpose, no longer correspond to reality and to the real sentiments of the group, but that the latter has not yet been able to substitute new representations for them. For, like structures, collective representations have a rise and fall. It is relevant to note here the "sociological" success of certain works of literature such as *La Nouvelle Héloïse* or *Werther* which give expression to the prevailing sensibility and so to the collective representation of their time. And yet such books, which in their day swept all Europe, leave the modern reader cold.

The fact is that collective representations are to a great extent based on man's experience, particularly his daily experience in his familiar surroundings: the scenery he looks at, the countries he visits, the food he eats, the dangers he fears—his daily encounter with nature in his work and craft. Ideology is not based on technology but always bears a relation to it. Human ideals are always to some degree an extrapolation of reality, in the way that the Mohammedan Paradise is the oasis dreamt of by the Bedouin. Even our knowledge of profound and permanent truths is conditioned by our human experience. Just as the child's conception of God differs from the old man's, so too the Middle Ages did not imagine him as a watchmaker (like Voltaire) or a Grand Architect (like the Freemasons). Collective representations also derive from scientific and philosophical systems which have become widespread through education, but the findings embodied in these systems continually need to be re-examined and hence there must be a reappraisal of the systems themselves and consequently of the collective representations.

Behaviour and custom

Collective representations give rise to common patterns of behaviour, attitudes and conduct. For instance, ceremonial forms of politeness are affected by the group's particular conception of man, of hospitality and of relative rank: they vary from one period or culture to another, while retaining certain common features such as consideration for others, the desire to please them and to win their favour, and a sense of hierarchic structure. To take another example, we find the same variation in the case of modesty, a phenomenon which differs enormously from one age or culture to another. One tribe may go about almost entirely naked, while another will cover the body so completely as to veil even the mouth, like the Touareg. Yet we cannot say *a priori* which of the two is the more modest because modesty is not simply a question of dress; it is expressed in attitudes, words, the observance of certain "taboos". Courtesy and modesty, together with the social conventions they bring with them, mark a point of contact between personal, interpersonal and social—the last-mentioned being the predominant element.

When patterns of behaviour become widespread among a number of groups they become incorporated into *custom*—a term which strictly speaking denotes a common set of patterns of conduct currently obtaining within a large collectivity such as a people or a civilization. Custom includes what our forefathers used to call "manners", indicating what one should do, or what one can or cannot do, depending on what is or is not "done". Take for example the length and various conditions of engagement or of family or national mourning, or the ceremonies connected with the attainment of the major stages of a man's life. In the East, and even in Spain, a guest had to express his gratitude to his host at the end of the meal by emitting a resounding belch—which would hardly be considered "the thing" to do in society today. An isolated detail like this is enough to suggest the almost infinite variety and relative character of custom. Where custom is concerned we may quote the old saying: "Truth this side of the Pyrenees is error the other". This does not mean to say that beneath this bewildering variety of detail there are not certain constants and quasi-constants common to all societies. While modesty differs in its various phenomena, the sense of modesty, closely connected with sexuality, is universal.

Custom implies imitation. We can classify the two major categories of custom, namely *usage* and *fashion*, according to the kind of imitation they imply.

A *usage* is the imitation, in time, of past precedent. One might formulate it as follows: such and such a thing is "done" because it has always been done so. "Always" is a relative term here because of course there was a time when the usage first started, and even now it is continually being modified, even if imperceptibly. "Always" in fact means simply "within living memory" or at least within the speaker's memory. The influence of usage is particularly marked in those societies and civilizations which ethnologists call *traditional*, where knowledge is handed down by oral tradition and common law prevails. Indeed the term "tradition" is to a certain degree synonymous with usage, although the idea of tradition implies not only continuity but also a dynamic vitality which usage does not necessarily involve. By methods of transmission which remain mysterious, usage is particularly strong in infant societies: it can be seen at work in their play, in their dance, in their story-telling. To sum up, usage is to society what habit is to the person: it is social habit.

Fashion is imitation not in time but in space: it is something essentially fleeting and ephemeral; in extreme cases it can arise, spread and disappear all within an instant. If usage is a deep current, fashion is a ripple on the surface. It might be formulated in this way: such and such a thing is done because everybody does it. Again "everybody" is a relative term here, meaning simply a large number of people in a particular milieu. The most obvious and widespread example of fashion is, of course, women's fashions. But in fact all activities have their fashions: literature, the arts, politics, even the sciences. Mussolini's "blackshirts" started a worldwide political fashion for shirts. Even vocabulary is affected by fashion, and every generation has its particular key-words like our own "efficient" or "effective". In our urban civilization, with the uprooting that it involves, fashion tends to prevail over usage without, however, completely supplanting it—witness such curious revivals as the choice of May 1st, an immemorial festival going back to primitive fertility rites, as the feast day of our "workers'" civilization.

In the realm of custom a major part is played by women. As educators of the very young it is women who pass on tradition, and also, because they are more anxious to please than men, they are more given to imitation in following usages or fashions. There is a division of labour, so to speak: men are concerned with institutions, with constructing, while women are concerned with custom, with living.

Within a global society there is a certain community of customs, but the latter are varied and shaded according to different milieux and sub-cultures. The customs of Stepney are not those of Belgravia, and those of Wigan are not those of Tunbridge Wells. The Londoner follows the customs of London, England and Western culture, but in addition to these there are "special" customs particular to the different sections of London society.

Mentalities and opinion

Collective representations and customs together go to form mentalities and opinion.

Mentality is a useful term: in its very vagueness it denotes something impressive, indefinable and often imperceptible, for it eludes detailed analysis, and yet it is an indispensable concept, denoting the set of beliefs, values, attitudes and behaviour which characterizes the members of a particular group. Every group develops its particular psychology and consequently its particular mentality.

The term "opinion" denotes something more precise and at the same time more elusive, belonging to the intellectual order. Opinion is the reaction of the group to an external challenge which brings into play its system of values. Based on the general mentality, it differs from it because it presupposes not only fundamental beliefs and customs but also judgements of fact, be it only an awareness of the challenge, and judgements of value which are expressed in words or attitudes. In a global society it is called "public opinion". Opinion is much more easy to analyse and even to calculate than mentality. Particular opinions of a small group can be discovered by means of sociometry and measured in terms of psychograms and sociograms, while those of a macro-group can be discovered by the soundings of a Gallup poll. Whether these methods are infallible is quite another matter, but there is no doubt that more results are obtained in this way than by pure intuition.

Fact and law

It can happen that custom conflicts with the law, even to the point of nullifying it, but often it helps in the making of law or in determining it through jurisprudence, which has to take it into account. Institutions too presuppose law, in so far as it brings them into being or sanctions the existence of pre-existing structures.

Law, therefore, is something pre-eminently social. While it would be presumptuous to judge a society on its legal code—there is a great difference, for instance, between the Soviet legal code and the Soviet way of life—it is impossible to know or to understand a society without taking into account its laws. Compare, for instance, the articles concerned with the family in the Code Napoléon with the contents of the Family legislation promulgated in 1939: there you can measure the difference between two epochs of French social life. Legislation is indicative of society by what it contains and also by what it leaves out, particularly if one takes into account not just the law itself but its applications, decrees, resolutions and jurisprudence.

For while law is not, as some would have it, simply the ratification of certain social facts, endorsing a combination of purely political and economic forces, it is closely bound up with actually existing society. To a certain extent all law starts from actual fact, either in recognizing its existence or defining and determining its essential elements in juridical terms; or in developing fact to its full perfection in accordance with the prevailing mentality; or, inversely, by undertaking to eliminate a fact which seems to be a nuisance or a danger, or to restrict and correct it, or to forestall some of its consequences; or finally in so far as law tries to introduce a new fact into the categories established by time-honoured usage, for intellectual convenience and in keeping with its marked conservative tendency. The legislation of the last century concerning the limited companies of commerce and industry ratified the existence and recognized the procedures of industrial capitalism and yet at the same time succeeded in standardizing these procedures and tried to provide against their possible abuse. Today concerns of a new "profit-sharing" type are only being slowly and painfully integrated into a system which has become traditional, and recourse must be made to legal artifice in order to make fact correspond to law and law to fact. Again, the theory of property established by the Civil Code becomes meaningless when it has to be applied to the nationalized enterprises of modern times, although in relation to literary, artistic and scientific copyright it continues to have effects never imagined by the original legislator.

Similarly all social or political, public or semi-public law, and to a certain extent the private law which is inevitably affected by them, have the effect of sanctioning the combinations of forces which they try as far as they can to balance. Law, which is a moral power, cannot ignore these forces, which are physical powers, whether it grants them legal recognition or whether it curbs their excesses or even crushes them. The development of industrial legislation within industrial and capitalist societies and its gradual embodiment in social legislation is due to the increased numerical and cohesive force of the working class, and also because, as the ranks of the wage-earners have grown, so the working-class mentality has slowly but surely pervaded the general mentality of society. Historically the progress of industrial law goes hand in hand with the progress of the trades unionism.

However, while sanctioning fact and endorsing combinations of forces, the law also helps to modify these facts and forces in so far as it rationalizes them, provides them with an institutional framework and gives them a sense of direction. All legislation in fact corresponds to particular conceptions of society and of the common good, which in turn correspond to a particular conception of the direction society should take, which in turn is bound up with a particular conception of society, of man and of the world. The Code Napoléon which under the inspiration of Portalis gave the French middle classes an organized structure presupposed a middle-class ideal which was to permeate the French mentality, including even those milieux outside the middle classes, and was to be propagated throughout Europe and the entire world. Law is at once the conscience and the consciousness of society.

The uniqueness of the social phenomenon

The foregoing analysis reveals the specific uniqueness of the social phenomenon, a synthesis which cannot be reduced to the diverse elements which it incorporates and unites.

Following the normal tendency of the human mind, which tries to reduce the unknown to the known, the new to the old, and succumbing also to the temptation of the nineteenth-century thinkers who, carried away by their enthusiasm for the natural sciences, sought to explain the superior in terms of the inferior and the complex in terms of the simple, the social sciences attempted at the beginning to reduce the social to the physical or biological. The result was what Auguste Comte called "social physics". The organicists talked of the "social organism" and the Darwinians saw society in terms of evolution and the struggle for existence. Later came the attempt, notably that of Freud, to reduce sociology to psychology, explaining social facts in terms of individual psychology.

All these attempts have proved failures. Social life of course has its own laws, but as Joseph Vialatoux has pointed out, the term law is misleading if one claims to transpose it directly from the realm of physics to that of sociology or even economics. It is an analogical, not a univocal term: social laws are no more connected with physical than with juridical laws. Again, society is something organic, admittedly, but its organization is not that of the animal organism—in this case, comparison is particularly misleading. Social facts are sometimes presented mathematically in terms of graphs and equations, but this presentation is in no sense an explanation: pan-mathematicism would be as valueless as all the other heterogeneous explanations because while mathematics is sufficiently adaptable to be able to symbolize quality it cannot explain it. Such a presentation has its advantages perhaps, but it also brings with it certain disadvantages, as Sorokin has recently shown—particularly the presentation with pseudo-scientific trappings which sets such a bait for the naïve. Again, it is permissible to speak of a social body, but on the understanding that the term is analogical and perhaps even metaphorical. Similarly we may talk about a collective psychology, but the term is specified by its epithet and is consequently quite distinct from individual psychologies: it affects and is affected by the latter without there being any confusion between them.

To this we should add that the purely relational being of society gives it a special position, not as a mental category, an abstraction, but endowed with a concreteness which is proper to it in the hierarchy of organic beings. The social fact is a human fact and as such it bears the imprint of man's uniqueness, the uniqueness of one who lives in cities and by his intelligence discovers relations which he can utilize, destroy or modify of his own free will.

Are social facts things?

In spite of Durkheim, who must be given his due for bringing out the specific uniqueness of the social fact, social facts are not "things". One might have supposed this already from the distinction ordinary language makes between "beings" and "things", implying that a thing is simply and solely an object, an inanimate and unconscious reality, completely at the mercy of exterior forces. A relational being, whose life involves values, ends and free choices, could not be treated as a thing.

On the other hand, if, in saying that social facts are things, we mean that the social sciences should study them with the impartiality and objectivity which are taken for granted in the natural sciences; if we mean that the researcher must set aside the inherited prejudices of his own milieu, must always keep in mind the uniqueness of the social fact and the distinction between the social sciences, art and morality—in a sense the statement is true, but we must define our terms clearly. However, it must be realized that impartiality and objectivity of the kind required are difficult and sometimes impossible to attain. A revolution, even that of the Gracchi in Republican Rome, cannot be studied in the same way as a crystallization or volcanic eruption; nor a religion, even that of the Bororos or Onas, in the same way as a culture medium or the respiratory system of a whale; nor can Inca society or the Jesuit settlements in Paraguay be looked at like an ant heap. For in every case though the scene is set in the past or in a distant land, behind it can be seen the shadow of the present and the immediate situation in which I find myself more or less involved and which inevitably obscures my judgement. Can a materialist and a religious believer look at ancient paganism with the same eyes? Their observations may perhaps concur if they are completely faithful to the facts but they will differ as soon as they start to interpret those facts. Even demographic or economic figures are not just figures: as Lucien Romier used to put it, they are flesh and blood in so far as they stand for men's labour and sustenance. Once the social sciences leave behind infra-social, and apply themselves to strictly social, phenomena they begin to pose the same problems as the historical sciences: in fact the two should work closely together.

Social facts are like things in so far as they are facts, but unlike them in so far as they are human facts.

The social sciences

The social sciences were as slow to understand this uniqueness and humanity inherent in the object of their study as to become aware of their own originality and consequent autonomy, particularly since they grew up in a positivist atmosphere which led them to take the natural sciences as their model. Only a few sociologists, like Montesquieu, de Tocqueville and Paul Bureau, remained untouched by this atmosphere. Even those as influential as Auguste Comte and Karl Marx, or Le Play and Tourville, have been affected by it to some extent. Hence the endless disputes about methodology which have been so prominent in the history of the social sciences. The other tendency has been for the latter to incline towards the moral sciences, a tendency evident in the term "moral and political sciences". Here there is a confusion between science and the techniques or arts, or between positive and normative science. It is only recently that the social sciences have reached their first stage of maturity in specifying their object, nature and methods in accordance with the realities which come inside the scope of their study.

From now on they are to be classified among the human sciences, as opposed to the natural sciences or the mathematical sciences. That is to say, on the one hand they reach conclusions which are of a different type to those obtained by the natural sciences and go no further than probability and the law of averages, while on the other hand they only have recourse to experiment in the analogical sense of experience, limited by the conditions which always govern any experimentation with human beings.

The social sciences are many in number, some of them general, others particular and specialized.

First of the more general sciences is *sociology*, which concerns itself with the whole field of social phenomena: social forms and structures, the relations between them and their effects upon individuals. Secondly there is *collective* or *social psychology*, which studies the feelings and behaviour of men within the group, over and above purely interpersonal activity. (None of these tentative definitions claims to be complete or even fully accurate: this is not the place to define or to attempt a critique of the social sciences.) Sociology and collective psychology are complementary and any full-scale explanation must take them both into account. Sociology is not *the* science of man but its very generality makes it what someone has aptly called a science of encounters and limits.

The social sciences with particular objects include *economics*, which deals with the phenomena consequent on the production and exchange of useful commodities; *demography*, which is concerned with the quantitative problems of population; *ethnography* or *cultural anthropology*, the study of so-called primitive societies and cultures; *folklore*, which concentrates on the survivals of primitive tradition within contemporary society; and finally the various political sciences.

These sciences, and the results obtained from them, can be the basis for means of collective action undertaken in the service of economic, political or social arts which will in turn further moral ends related to human action.

But social techniques, like all techniques, do not themselves possess their own ends. And if the social sciences are neither techniques nor arts, still less are they to be classified as moral philosophies. They are positive sciences, concerned with observing, describing and explaining, and as such they express themselves in the indicative mood, while moral philosophy, as a normative science, prefers the imperative and optative. The question remains, is it possible to conceive of a social morality and, if so, how will it relate to the human sciences? This will be the subject of a later chapter.

CHAPTER II

THE DIRECTION OF SOCIAL LIFE

Man is a traveller here below. He follows his temporal road from the cradle to the grave, but in dying he is only crossing over finally from the shore of time to that of eternity. Even in his earthly journey he is at once part of time and part of eternity, for out of time, his time, he makes his eternity. His journey is a pilgrimage. Thus the human race pursues its destiny, initiated by the first erect and rational creature and proceeding towards an inevitable end—beginning and end alike shrouded in mystery. Even the universe, the stage on which the human individual and the human species appear, derives its movement from the creative impetus which gives it its being. Time, because it is time, will come to an end: it proceeded from eternity and will return into eternity. Person, species and universe, all go forward in time towards eternity, that is to say their progress is towards God, who is Eternity itself, and in God, who is omnipresent.

Man's journey, then, has a meaning and a destination. The human caravan is wending its way towards an oasis, and at the same time every pilgrim who leaves it on the way has found the end of his allotted stage. Neither pilgrims nor caravan, then, can go astray; just as the caravan driver knows his destination and finds his way by the stars or by following tracks, so man individually and socially regulates his progress by certain landmarks and standards; in order to progress he must comply with a law within his own nature, a law to which he is subject along with all other creatures of the universe. It says: "Become what you are, a person, a being at once animal and spiritual, subjecting the inferior to the superior parts of your nature as means are subjected to ends, bringing your human nature to fruition in fulfilling your vocation which has its special contribution to make to the harmony of the universe; using the time which is granted you and within which you are given a unique place, to prepare for your eternal consummation. The law of your being is one of movement, fulfilment and progress. Movement, because here you have no abiding city, but each of the dwelling-places where you find shelter on the stages of your journey offers an opportunity for realizing yourself, and consequently your personal destiny is inseparable from your destiny as a member of society, one who journeys in a group and who builds houses and cities".

Thus in his own nature, in his vocation to fulfil himself in and through his social conditions, man can discern that basic imperative: Do good and avoid evil, which the scholastics called synderesis—a precept which implies man's specific distinction, the ability to choose between all the human acts which proceed from his freedom. Applying this principle to human relations he draws two further conclusions: do not do to others what you would not have them do to you, and do to others what you would have them do to you. The Christian Gospel sums up these two axioms in that formula which contains the fullness of the law: love God above all things and love your neighbour as yourself for the love of God. Never has the fundamental rule of morality been more clearly and forcibly expressed than this. But love is infinite, for the measure of love is to be boundless. And in his nature man finds not only obligations and imperatives but also impulses and aspirations for good which beget a continual restlessness in him, a constant desire for what is new and better. The person seeks to fulfil himself, therefore, but he is also bound to transcendence, and this transcendence is indeed the condition of his fulfilment. These interior rules of action, these laws, dispositions, behaviour, obligations and aspirations together constitute what we know as morality, the science which governs human acts.

A human morality is inevitably a social morality, since human nature implies sociability and "sociality". Whether it is simply a social morality is another question: quite rightly, moralists make a distinction between social morality and personal morality—not to mention interpersonal morality. Starting with moral principles man draws certain logical conclusions from them by rational deduction and by induction from personal or collective experience. The person is always placed in a particular situation and each situation elicits human acts, in other words behaviour governed by morality. For the most part these situations are social: even when personal or interpersonal they are played against a social background. These situations and the confrontation between imperatives and facts result in conclusions which the person formulates in terms of "can" and "ought". What he can do is moral *right*, a kind of law which in its entirety constitutes the natural law whether primary or derived—completed and specified by experience. What he ought to do is *obligation*, duty, which in its complete set of rules constitutes morality. Right and obligation are logically and psychologically complementary: a man's obligation to do something implies a corresponding right to do it; his rights involve corresponding obligations towards others and other people's rights involve obligations towards him. It is contradictory therefore to admit the existence of a natural morality while denying the existence of a natural law: such a contradiction can only be explained by prejudice or reaction against misuse of the concept of natural law. Complementary, therefore, even if not agreeing in every particular, morality and natural law are evidently capable of progress. They do not undergo any essential change in as much as they are bound up with human nature, but they evolve according to the logic of their essence, by being specified and added to, by being renewed and enriched, by giving a universal formulation to what began by being a personal initiative and transforming what may have been initially an aspiration into terms of obligation. Morality is also an art of living, the science of human happiness, for happiness is nothing other than personal fulfilment, and consequently social morality will be the art of collective happiness, or to be more precise, since society is only a relational being, the art of the social conditions of human happiness.

Social morality, therefore, is the science which governs the conduct of man in society. If we see it in this light, we cannot regard it simply as governing personal actions as and when they impinge on society. That would imply an individualistic conception of society and would in effect reduce social causality to the status of occasional causality. No, social morality governs human actions in and upon society, which includes the construction, the preservation, the modification and the spirit of relational systems, institutions and customs, and consequently the mutual relations obtaining between societies in so far as they are susceptible of being acted upon by personal will. Society itself cannot be the seat of moral conscience because it is not a subject, in the psychological and metaphysical sense of the word, and only becomes a legal subject through the legal fiction of the "moral person"—a term devised by analogy with the human person. The person, however, the adequate subject of conscience, acts through, with, in and upon society.

These moral, metaphysical and theological observations are not contradicted *a priori* by the positive study of social life, which shows that every society produces its own morality, a code of action and definition of happiness, an ordered system of values and ends depending on a transcendent end—either metaphysically transcendent, beyond time and history, or what we would call semi-transcendent, situated not above but ahead, in the historical future (like the idea of progress or the Communist society).

We have still to see whether there is any connection and correspondence between the ontological and the phenomenal order. Is ontology no more than ideology, and are phenomena made up simply of illusions? In other words, does a social morality exist? Or if there is such a thing as morality, is it simply a personal morality, or simply a social morality? We have partially answered these questions above, but they must be treated further and with more precision.

The genesis of moral conscience

It is useful here to study the genesis of moral conscience in the person and the group.

Just as a small child becomes aware of its existence under the effect of the external world, and becomes conscious of its personality by learning to distinguish between self and not-self and then between the self as an object and as a subject, so too it develops a personal moral conscience under the effect of external and social influences. Initially these influences are strictly interpersonal, between the child and its mother, with whom it has formed one body and from whom it is gradually distinguished. However in fact society is present to the child *in* the mother, to the extent that the child's first education is an acculturation and an initiation into society, for as Margaret Mead has shown, even methods of suckling differ from one culture to another. Thus the mother adds to the child's ego and social super-ego which becomes part of his subconscious. The child also develops an awareness of morality, under the form of compulsion, by being physically constrained by his mother to perform certain actions, and under the form of aspiration, by the soon-awakened desire to please her. The notion of moral obligation comes later.

As he grows up and begins to explore the world, the child continues to be aware of the Thou-relationship which his mother has taught him but also discovers the *other*, or more precisely others—which include people like his father, brothers and sisters with whom he has a special Thou-relationship too.

In this confusing world of the "other" he discovers an important distinction, the distinction between things, which are objects, and beings, which are subjects, endowed like himself with sense and spirit. He finds that each of these categories poses different obligations for him, where propriety and politeness are concerned, for example. He advances, therefore, from a "thou" morality to an "other" morality, and then in the family community he becomes aware also of a "we", distinct from I, thou, you and he: thereupon he acquires a "we" morality, a social morality in fact. The notion of moral obligation properly speaking only begins to appear at the end of infancy, when the child is approaching the age of reason, when he is learning to distinguish between good and evil and between what he is forced to do, what he wants to do and what he is bound to do, and when he is being integrated into society through play, school and the companionship of other children. At this stage too the child becomes aware of his obligations towards himself, to the extent that he grows out of an initial "autism" and attains a reflex knowledge of himself. To education finally is due the formation of his moral conscience—a process which is never-ending.

In sum, the child discovers social morality by means of interpersonal morality and then personal morality by means of social morality. As he makes these discoveries so he builds up a living morality, learning to distinguish as his reason develops, until he reaches the state of adulthood.

Within societies and communities the development of moral conscience takes rather a different form. It seems to start with an unquestioning attachment to the group "we", an attitude of complete loyalty and conformity. In this way the child identifies himself with his family or later with his companions, and in primitive societies a man is inseparably linked with his clan or family. Thus the group appears as the very source of morality, which becomes inseparable from a wholehearted commitment to the group. Gradually, however, the person declares his independence of the group and begins to exercise his critical judgement in its regard. Soon he becomes conscious of an obligation to modify it in its spirit, structure or workings: he discovers the existence of other, higher groups of which his own group forms a part or which are quite distinct from it: he becomes aware of others not just as individuals but collectively, and thereby he discovers new ties, new likes and dislikes, new obligations.

Moral progress in a society often begins with the initiative of certain persons or small groups who break away from accepted convention. Subjected at first to hostility and unpopularity they slowly gain a following and their influence spreads until finally their ideas become current coin and their practice becomes general. Finally comes the sanction of statutory or common law. This process can be seen at work in many historical movements, such as those for the abolition of gladiatorial combat, ordeals, human sacrifice, judicial and private duelling, for the mitigation and later the abolition of slavery, for the replacement of polygamy by monogamy.

To sum up, moral conscience is developed in and through the group, but sooner or later the group conscience is altered and transformed by personal morality. Here again we are dealing with a concrete whole, where the possibility of distinctions does not mean dichotomy. Adopting the existentialist idea of "regard" or scrutiny, we might say that the person lives his life under the scrutiny of others, of the group, and that they contribute to the development of his moral conscience, while societies in their turn are subject to scrutiny by the person, who contributes to the formation of the general conscience. This account of the genesis of moral conscience would seem to indicate, therefore, that personal morality and social morality are inseparable, as inseparable as man the individual and man the social animal.

Morality and ethics

Nevertheless, the idea of social morality is rejected by many theorists, primarily of course by those who refuse to admit morality as such at all.

Some, like Lévy-Bruhl at one time, see morality as being simply a descriptive, analytical and positive science which examines and tries to explain the behaviour general in a given place and at a given time. This amounts to equating morality with social morality and at the same time denies the existence of morality or ethics as a normative science.

This theory, however, serves a useful purpose in reminding us that social morality cannot be, as it has too often been made out to be, simply a series of deductions, theorems, corollaries even, drawn from a preconceived notion of human nature. Morality is a normative science, certainly, but it is also a science of morals, in so far as the actual facts must be known and understood before there can be any moral judgement made and practical conclusions drawn. As we have seen, morality progresses only in so far as facts create problems which demand solutions. It is not a mere accident, therefore, that the French word *moraliste* can be applied equally to the moral philosopher and to the student of morals. Taparelli d'Azeglio was not simply being paradoxical in speaking of a natural law based upon facts. Morality cannot do without the social sciences.

On the other hand morality cannot be reduced simply to a science of morals without shirking the problem. Though idealists may ignore the fact, it cannot be denied that institutions and conventions subject the individual to psychological pressure, and that this coercion sometimes disguises itself as moral obligation. Even so, we still have to explain a series of transitions: the transition from the indicative to the imperative, from the external compulsion to the interior obligation, from doing or not doing something because it is not "done" to doing or not doing it because it ought or ought not to be done, and finally the transition from the particular obligation towards a particular individual or group to the universal obligation towards all men, towards mankind. And the key question, the vital riddle, concerns the intrinsic value of moral obligation. Is it valid only in relation to society, or does it have its own validity, consequent on man's very nature and destiny? Is it only valid within a particular institutional and moral context, or does it have an essential validity for all times, places and circumstances? If it imposes itself upon us, in whose name or by what right does it do so? No positive and phenomenal science can provide an answer to questions like these. Facts and appearances are not enough. In order to live, we must philosophize.

Social scientism

The idea of morality as a science of morals is ultimately derived from positivist philosophy. Other theories reject social morality in accordance with certain materialist notions which were fashionable in the last century. We use the term social scientism to describe them because they all regard the social sciences along the lines of the natural sciences and study social phenomena as they would study inanimate or inorganic natural phenomena.

For some, social phenomena are similar to physical phenomena—governed by rigorous laws, which are capable of experimental discovery and formulation. This "social physics" leaves no room for morality: morality, like free will, is simply an illusion, an epiphenomenon which cannot affect the turn of events for this is simply to be explained in terms of human atoms uniting and combining in accordance with fixed determinist laws.

For others, notably certain racialists, social phenomena belong to the biological order. They see society as an organism governed by strict laws of correlation, or again as a kind of jungle in which the laws of evolution—the struggle for life, survival of the fittest—prevail. Here the determinism is rather less pronounced. Though we must refrain from doing anything which, in the name of non-existent morality, might upset the operation of social physics, it is possible, according to certain eugenist and racialist theories, to use an accommodated social art to transform the jungle into a garden. This social husbandry, however, has nothing in common with morality.

Social physicism and social biologism often provide the foundation for what P. Albert Valensin used to call doctrines of force. This is not surprising, for physics and biology simply register the collisions and combinations of what are metaphorically called natural forces. These doctrines found their most brutally clear, if not their best, exponent in the German von Bernhardi, but their influence can be seen to a greater or less extent in much contemporary political ideology. Their most succinct expression is not the well-known slogan Might surpasses Right—which has the disadvantage of presupposing that Right objectively exists—but the simpler formula, Might is Right, which leads to the corollary that the one and only article of social morality is to possess the greatest strength.

Comparison is no substitute for reason. We are entitled to compare social facts to physical or biological facts, and to compare the human sciences to the natural sciences. But those who reduce the one to the other, annexing the superior to the inferior, and deny the specific uniqueness of the social, and hence of the human, fact, are basing themselves not on science but on some ready-made materialistic or pantheistic philosophy which we have the right to cross-examine. Man is not a stone, nor a tiger, but a man. This is paradoxically confirmed by the very fact that he erects these "physicist" or "biologist" theories, because they show him to be capable of induction and deduction, abstraction and generalization, even at the price of error. A purely animal or vegetable creature is not capable of intellectual error in the strict sense.

Furthermore, the inadequacy of these theories is often revealed in their contradictions. If men are simply atoms swept along by the current of a quasi-physical determinism, then how can haphazard interventions upset the natural operation of social laws? Either man is unable to intervene in the process of social physics and any such intervention is an illusion; or else he can intervene, in which case he is not determined, at least not completely determined. Even if he intervenes only to keep the natural operation going, he is intervening none the less, with an ulterior purpose. Again, if man is no more than a plant or a beast in the social jungle how can he set about cultivating that jungle? If he can so cultivate it, then he is doing so in order to impose a certain conception of order on it.

Similar contradictions are to be found in Marxist materialism and the physical determinism of certain liberals. How is one to reconcile the doctrine of materialism with the idea of dialectical evolution, an idea which implies some spiritual force at work? Again how can "scientific" socialism admit the desire for justice, which is a moral postulate? How does a freely-willed human action such as a revolution fit into the determinist theory of evolution?

The concept of natural law cannot be transferred or even transposed into the context of society because within this context the very terms law and nature take on a different meaning and dimension. The laws of history, to use a rather pretentious expression, have little in common with Justinian's laws, or the laws of organic correlation. What we call the laws of society are in fact no more than the statement of the recurrences, constants and consecutions which rule the average individual in a given context. What happened to the famous natural laws of the liberal economy, as soon as they went beyond the findings of common sense, as regards the relations between supply and demand in open and closed markets? And the sociologists and historians who have set themselves to formulate the so-called laws of history have so far agreed on nothing save some elementary conclusions from historical experience or on certain facts which they can state without being able to explain. As for the doctrines of force, they too ignore the specific uniqueness of man, forgetting that force is only effective in human action when it is used by the reason in order to attain certain ends, and ends presuppose values and hence morality. Again, to say that right often overcomes might is a commonplace of the pulpit, but it is quite another thing to say that right is might—all the more because not all human might or power is physical, and the man who is "in the right" thereby gains in psychological and moral power. The rejoinder might be that one can do anything with a bayonet except sit on it. Force without reason, *vis extra rationem*, is destructive and ruinous, it is simply blind violence. To put the world at the mercy of force is to abandon it to chance, and yet man cannot do this, for by virtue of his very nature he must rationalize reality. The doctrine of force corresponds to an essentially adolescent conception of human relations, the Superman idea. Ultimately, therefore, these theories of social scientism, bound up with scientific concepts that are now outdated, are to be regarded as cultural and irrational, rather than strictly intellectual phenomena: they are important not for their own merits so much as for their influence on collective representations.

Juridical positivism and political realism

The theories we have just outlined give rise to the doctrines, or rather the doctrinal tendencies, of juridical positivism and political realism.

What Pius XII called juridical positivism regards positive law, the law promulgated by political authority and interpreted by the bench, as the one and only source of law: it does not admit the existence of natural law. According to this theory the ultimate source of the law resides in the will of the Ruler, whether autocratic, oligarchic or democratic. In its extreme forms it even regards the judge as the instinctive and omnipotent interpreter of the general will: so it is with Nazi and Soviet law and, to a lesser extent with the "tribunals" which administer what is sometimes called "political justice".

Juridical positivism cannot be consistent unless it rejects the idea of social morality as well as that of natural law. In this event the will of the legislator becomes the exclusive source of law and morality, which is really a re-introduction of the doctrines of force. If, on the other hand, its advocates admit the existence of morality on the individual and social level it becomes difficult for them to deny the existence of a natural law consequent upon morality, to which positive law must conform itself as far as possible. In this case, if morality exists, it is hard to see why the legislator should be so privileged as to be exempted from the demands of a morality to which all human persons are subject: such an exemption would be flagrantly illogical.

Political realism, what the Germans call *Realpolitik*, also has both extreme and moderate forms. It may reject all morality as regards political ends and means and embrace a thorough-going Machiavellianism (we prescind from the question how far this term corresponds to what Machiavelli actually taught), in which case it is simply another variety of the doctrine of force. It can also appear in the more moderate form of authoritarianism or social pragmatism, in which case it does not question the existence of political morality but at the same time holds that in certain circumstances, given the gravity of the situation and the importance of what is at stake, a legitimate end justifies the use of any means, even if they are intrinsically immoral: what primarily matters is success. It is not difficult to see the dangers inherent in this attitude: even its moderate forms can so easily be turned to extremism. Yet the fact that it can be abused is no sufficient indictment of it: what condemns it is its logical incoherence. If we believe in moral imperatives then they are absolute, *a fortiori* in this particular case. Either we must take morality or else we must leave it. The axiom "He who wills the end wills the means" signifies that the means of action should be relative and proportionate to the end pursued, and consequently a legitimate end must be attained by legitimate means: exceptional situations may call for exceptional measures, as for example in the case of extreme necessity a man is not bound by the positive law of property, but never for measures which are intrinsically immoral.

Political realism, in fact, indicates a rather immature attitude, the attitude which tends to sacrifice slow results to immediate success, a long-term to a short-term policy. While invoking the criterion of efficiency it comes to measure the effectiveness of any given means by its immorality and the cleverness of a policy by its unscrupulousness. In this context much could be said about the cult of Talleyrand which is fashionable in certain French circles.

Moral individualism

Moral individualism is the exact opposite of the doctrines we have just been discussing. Whether they admit the existence of morality or not, for all practical purposes these doctrines base morality on society: for them there is no morality other than social morality, and personal or interpersonal obligations are in the last analysis obligations towards society, enforced by authority or opinion. For moral individualism, on the other hand, it is the individual who is the one subject and object of morality. Its advocates admit no other morality than individual morality. Yet in a roundabout way, the same conclusion emerges from their theories as from those of their opponents—the denial of social morality.

Social individualism has many forms, ranging in degree from rigid to moderate or crypto-individualistic.

In its more extreme form it is to be found in the doctrine of individualistic anarchism, expounded with rigorous logic by Stirner and later given more poetical and less precise expression by Nietzsche, Ibsen and other nineteenth-century writers. According to this doctrine, society constitutes a perpetual threat to the individual, on whom it unceasingly exerts an oppressive, coercive and degrading influence. The vocation of the individual, therefore, is to fulfil his own unique and inimitable self in spite of and if necessary in the teeth of his social conditions: he must go beyond good and evil and beyond morality, which is simply a social obstacle, instructive but irrelevant.

In its extreme form individualistic anarchism amounts to the same as the doctrines of force, except that it has its basis in the individual and not in the social authorities. It has something else in common with these doctrines, not immediately apparent and yet fundamental: they both share the same radical pessimism as regards the human condition, the same philosophical background of pantheism or materialism, the same intellectual anarchy, the same culpable ignorance of moral and juridical principles. There is a right-wing anarchism as well as a left-wing anarchism: Benvenuto Cellini and Caesar Borgia, Ravachol and Hitler, have more in common than the uninitiated think. Both theoretically and practically the doctrine is untenable; theoretically because it denies man's social nature, which is to contradict the evidence; practically because its logic leads finally to suicide, prison or the mental asylum.

More frequently it takes the attenuated form of liberal individualism. In France, we can see traces of this in the writings of Alain, with their theory of "the citizen versus the authorities". The citizen, taken as an individual, is good: authority, whether legal or effective authority, is, if not bad at least dangerous, always open to abuse. The attitude of the citizen, therefore, towards authority and towards the societies which the possessors of authority organize and represent, must be one of guarded mistrust. There is indeed some truth in all this: authority is only too prone to abuse its power, and consequently it must be subject to limitation and control. But as a systematic doctrine it tends to emphasize man's individuality at the expense of his social nature and so to give an unbalanced, depersonalized picture; there is also the danger that it may, by confusing individualism with egoism, foster a civic indifferentism.

Another form of moral individualism is that version of existentialism which has developed the Situation Ethic. Since man, who is the perfectly free creature, himself assigns an essence to his existence, it follows that human nature is a meaningless concept: moral action is simply free action, unaffected by any extrinsic or intrinsic rule. Man is always placed in a situation, and it is his free response to the demands of the situation which form his essence and his morality. The only morality, therefore, is the morality of situation. This subjectivism ultimately amounts to the same as anarchic individualism: it rejects not just social morality but the whole concept of morality as a complex of permanent and universal obligations. It is based on a confusion between the prepositions "of" and "in": every morality is *in* a situation, because of course it must meet the demands of particular situations which, though perhaps similar, are never identical, since every person and every event is unique; it is not thereby a morality *of* situation, however, because moral decisions, which are reached by the practical judgement, are not simply a matter of a particular free will encountering a particular situation but imply a reference to certain principles, which are interpreted by the individual conscience. In fact situation morality does not so much restore man to his liberty as it abandons him to his instincts, passions and humours, if not to the mercy of fate: it ignores man's specific differential, his reason.

Certain forms of social individualism are religious in origin. For example, some religions are so preoccupied with the idea of personal salvation that they leave out of account the salvation of society. Thus the practical rejection of social morality can be accompanied by a code of personal morality which is sometimes of an exacting and even puritanical standard and often has an ascetical or mystical character. Those religions, for instance, which teach the doctrine of the transmigration of souls will therefore explain the social situation of an individual as the effect of his previous life, in accordance with a kind of spiritual determinism: such situations cannot be other than they are, and it is impossible to alter them. These religions often involve a caste system for the general mass, and monastic or eremitical life for the chosen few. Then there is Lutheranism which not only distinguishes but entirely separates the temporal and the spiritual, which is seen as identical with the interior: thus the "world", the social and political world, is abandoned to Satan and the spirits of evil, and the citizen must simply obey the authorities in all things temporal and live in accordance with his vocation, or *Beruf*. Similar aberrations appeared in eighteenth and nineteenth-century Catholicism, through the infiltration into the Church of bourgeois individualism, for which the "one thing necessary" is personal salvation. These mistaken ideas explain the submissive acceptance by some Catholics of the theory of the "divine right" of kings and later of the "natural laws" of economic liberalism. Among certain Protestant sects of a liberal tendency religious individualism, derived from the principle of free thought, asserts the absolute sovereignty of the individual conscience: without actually denying the existence of social morality it subordinates its applications to the subjective decisions of individual conscience, which is free to reject the decisions of authority, either in particular or in general.

This moral and religious individualism also finds expression in certain naïve theories of social action and reform. There is, for example, the famous argument of Brunetière: social problems = moral problems, which = religious problems—overlooking the fact that these problems overlap and interrelate without being identical. Or there is the theory which makes social reform almost entirely dependent on the self-reformation of individuals, instead of regarding the latter simply as an indispensable condition of the former. We are all familiar with this kind of argument: if everybody had a sense of civic responsibility . . . if every employer and employee did his duty . . . if everyone lent a hand to his neighbour. . . . The answer of course is Yes, but even supposing all drivers were geniuses and saints, that would not be a reason for abolishing road signs and doing away with the Highway Code.

Personal conscience and social life

Moral individualism of the religious type is right to stress the rôle of the individual conscience but it goes wrong in over-emphasizing its importance and above all in creating a false picture of it. Here, certainly, it could learn something from the "science of morals".

It is an elementary moral principle that everyone is bound to follow his conscience, even where it is wrong. Yet this is precisely the point: the conscience can be wrong—indeed we can go even further and say, without undue pessimism, that every conscience is always to a greater or lesser extent distorted at least on some occasions. Besides, we have already seen for ourselves the way in which the moral conscience develops: it is not a kind of spiritual instinct, an interior voice speaking with infallible authority, but a rational and emotional complex to which personal, interpersonal and social elements all contribute: it uses the knowledge thus acquired and the habits (or, more precisely, the *habitus*) thus formed to make practical judgements demanded by the needs of a situation. In short, it puts into practice that virtue concerned with the intellect and will which was known by the now debased name of prudence. There is room for error, then, not only in the activity of the conscience but in its very development, and here in fact error actually occurs.

A given individual conscience is not simply the product of its social conditions, as some extremists would maintain, it is to some extent also the effect of these conditions. Every conscience is affected by social pressures which sometimes wear the disguise of moral obligations, and again every conscience is influenced in its practical decisions by collective representations together with the prejudices they embody, and by current values together with the arbitrary and irrational elements they involve. This effect of society upon the conscience appears particularly in those actions which are both moral and social, for instance, in matters relating to honour or modesty.

Also, all conflict between personal conscience and social life involves a certain ambiguity: the source of the conflict may lie in what specifically pertains to the person, in his thoughts and hopes, or in what he takes over from society—the prejudices which characterize his particular age and milieu. The nature of the conflict can only be clearly seen by referring to a rule which embraces the individual conscience and society alike, and this rule is nothing other than social morality. We cannot assert *a priori*, as the extreme socialists would have us do, that the claims of the group must always take precedence over those of the person nor as the individualists would maintain, that the claims of the person must always take precedence over those of the group. Each in fact must be given its due: this is in accordance with the nature of man and of society and with the divine Will which has constituted them.

The disadvantages of double morality

What emerges from our argument is the impossibility of maintaining two moralities, one valid for the individual and the other for society or, to be more accurate, the impossibility of suggesting that morality is exclusively concerned with the individual alone or with society alone.

To say that morality is simply and solely social morality is to subordinate relational being to subsistent being, to deny the tendency to autonomy which is characteristic of the human person, to obliterate the importance of the conscience, to ignore the domain of personal and interpersonal activity, and at the same time to undermine the force of moral obligation which becomes identified with the immediate pressure of the group and disappears in the shifting flux of social change.

On the other hand, to identify morality with personal morality is to deny the relational being of society, existing apart from man, and to impoverish the concept of man himself, disregarding the social side of his nature, to ignore his tendency towards expansion and heteronomy and finally to subvert moral obligation by making it depend upon the subjective inspiration of the individual conscience.

Besides, the doctrine of double morality is obviously quite untenable in practice: if a person believes that the only morality is social morality and that morality is the invention of society, sooner or later he will come to doubt morality itself and this doubt will manifest itself in his behaviour: he will yield only to the pressure of force or opinion, he will be deprived of inward strength and stability and become irresponsible and vacillating. If, on the other hand, he believes only in individual morality he will inevitably come to behave in an a-social or anti-social way which will result in a kind of depersonalization: again he will lose his inward strength and outward stability for he will follow every selfish impulse and every prompting of passion as if it were the voice of conscience. When, abandoned as he is to the almost systematic pursuit of immorality, he is called upon by authority to put into practice those moral virtues which are necessary to the life of society, then he will be rudely awakened to the fact that morality is one and indivisible. Double morality is as fatal to morality as double truth is to truth. There are not two moralities but one single human morality, diversified in its structure and yet, like man himself, a unity. Alternatively, there is no morality, only chaos, absurdity and despair.

Social determinism

We have examined the corrupting effects upon morality of extreme socialism and extreme individualism, leaving on one side the more moderate and tentative theories which approximate to them, but our critical task is not completed until we have answered the fundamental question, is society subject to determinism—in the sense which the term has for the natural sciences? If such determinisms exist then obviously social morality is an impossibility.

It must be understood, of course, that we are speaking of *social* determinisms as such, not of physical or biological determinisms which, as we hope to have shown above, do not apply to social phenomena because they belong to quite a different order. This order is the human order which, of course, is part of nature, in the wide sense of the term, but differs from it if we understand nature as including unreasoning and unreflecting creatures as opposed to rational beings.

Nor are we concerned here with specifically psychological determinisms, since all explanations of society in terms of individual psychology are inadequate. It should be noted here that the whole question of social determinism does not affect the question of personal free will. Relational being may be determined by certain factors which do nothing to alter the nature of subsistent being; if, of course, we believe that individuals are determined then it follows that society is determined, but the converse does not hold necessarily, since it is not the entire group which is determined, properly speaking, but the cross-section of the group. This is how insurance companies make their calculations: the number of road accidents during a Whitsun weekend can be predicted almost to within a matter of hundreds, and yet this forecast still leaves the individual driver free to accept or refuse that extra drink which causes the accident. As we have already shown, social laws are only concerned with the average percentage.

The idea of social determinism, of course, does not appeal to idealist or "spiritual" philosophers, to moralists or to reformers, who reject it out of hand. They like to consider the field of social phenomena as passive or at least susceptible of human free will, and they reduce social causality to simple material causality. Unfortunately, things are not quite so simple as that. Experience and man's own composite nature point to the existence of strictly social determinisms which are quite separate from any natural determinisms. These social determinisms, however, do not affect the principles of social morality because the exercise of free will and the freedom to remain impartial, though limited or conditioned, are not suppressed by them. They do not relate to the group in its entirety but to the group taken on average and they are essentially limited, relative and conditional: unlike determining factors of a physical or biological kind (such as heredity or race) their effect upon individuals or groups is not direct, but indirect, mediated by individual or collective representations. They can be formulated in these terms: all things being equal, it is highly probable that given particular conditions a particular result will follow. We are not dealing with certainties, therefore, still less with mathematical certainties, but with consecutions, with matters of high probability, and the element of causality which they contain is difficult to determine. Moreover, they are at least partly dependent on human free will which can provide or withhold the necessary conditions, and can abolish or modify them or curtail their effects. There can be no such thing as an absolute determinism in the social order. To realize this we have only to consider the current phenomenon of the "social rebel". The rebel is one who contracts out of society, wholly or partially. The ordinary rebel, such as the deserter, the bandit or the conscientious objector contents himself with rejecting a consequence of social life, but the radical rebel rejects society entirely, whether he is a reformer who thinks in terms of reshaping society slowly and from within, or the revolutionary who wants to use external and more brutal means, or the anarchist who cuts himself off altogether. This phenomenon of the social rebel, then, points to the limitations of social determinism. The fact that the rebel frequently gathers a group around himself is simply a consequence of his social nature.

Having defined our terms, we may distinguish three major categories of determinism: determinism of environment, determinism of average behaviour and determinism of inertia.

Environmental determinism is a result of the animal element in human nature which is sensitive to the physical, chemical or biological influences of its surroundings. The first imperative of social life is to live, and, in order to live, to adapt oneself. Soil, subsoil, climate, orology, hydrology, the facility or difficulty of communications—all these conditions, which form the subject of human geography, affect man both as an individual and in society. The African jungle and the polar wastes, the desert and the seaport city—all give rise to a different type of society. The soil will produce foodstuffs: "Tell me what you eat and I will tell you what manner of man you are." The wealth of the subsoil provides the resources for industry. The climate determines rhythms of living and working. Geographical position will facilitate or hinder commerce. Moreover, all exploitation of nature by man involves a technology, and the demands of technique have their effect upon human relations, for instance, upon forms of authority and property. Natural environment conditions techniques, which in turn condition relations to work, which in turn condition social relations. Finally, all these factors together will condition different views of life, cultures and civilizations. There are some societies so closely bound up with their environment that to attempt to modify them is to risk their destruction. In this context one has only to think of the Eskimos, the Maoris and the people of Tierra del Fuego.

Environmental determinism, however definite, is never absolute. The conditionings we have described represent not causes but conditions. Many errors concerning human determinism in fact stem from a confusion between the different categories of causes, or from a confusion between a cause, a conditioning factor and what the scholastics used to call a *removens prohibens*. Conditioning processes are reciprocal and work both ways: cultures react on institutions and techniques, and vice versa. Moreover, in some cases a man may leave his environment out of account, either inadvertently or deliberately. Some tribes will die out rather than change their methods of obtaining food, while others refuse to use what nature offers them in their surroundings because of cultural taboos. There are island peoples who practise neither navigation nor trade, and again there are collectivities possessing a rich subsoil which are too ignorant, unwilling or unable to exploit it. Finally, by means of technique man reacts on his environment and transforms it: here we have only to think of the effect of domestic animals and of cultivated plants. To over-emphasize environmental determinism is to incur the charge of geographical materialism which Charles Gide brought against Edmond Demolins and to fall into the error of Marxist pan-economicism.

The *determinism of average behaviour* relates to man's psychological nature, to his instincts and reason, to the workings of his conscious and unconscious mind. Experience goes to show that, given particular premises, in certain conditions the average percentage of men within groups and the average percentage of the groups themselves behave analogously, either because their instincts impel them to live and reproduce themselves and have the same side-effects, or because their rational powers operate according to a logic which is substantially identical in spite of accidental differences of time and place; or, finally, in accordance with a pre-logic which is rooted in their subconscious. This kind of determinism is particularly noticeable when we are dealing with infra-social phenomena, such as the crowd or assembly. In the strictly social domain, it provides a basis for the scales of premiums and prestations which are calculated by insurance companies. As we have already said, it does not affect the principle of individual freedom. The number of suicides within a group may remain more or less constant, but this does not mean that each individual suicide is constrained to take his own life by an inevitable determinism. It is as if a sort of general tendency was abroad which may or may not affect each particular individual, depending on his willingness or unwillingness. Contrary to what one might expect, the operation of personal liberty is not necessarily opposed to this determinism, since free actions are directed by reasons which work analogously. A reasonable man may predict, with a considerable degree of probability, the behaviour of another reasonable man by putting himself in his place, as they say, or getting into his skin; what he cannot predict is the behaviour of the insane, mentally sick, psychotic or neurotic man, unless he happens to have a thorough knowledge of the man and his sickness, for the behaviour of the unbalanced is erratic. Nor can he predict the behaviour of the supra-normal man, the genius, hero, or saint because this goes beyond the ordinary norms.

These last remarks indicate the limitations of the determinism of average behaviour. Since it is only concerned with averages it is restricted to the realm of probability. There is always a number of individuals who are left unaffected by the general tendency, whether because they are sub-normal—criminals, perverts, the brutish or the insane—super-normal, or *inner-directed*, guiding themselves by the light of their own consciences. Even when a group seems to have achieved unanimity, for example in a great national crisis, this unanimity does not go very deep. Even the impulses of instinct can in fact be resisted: in spite of the instinct for self-preservation men will let themselves die of hunger, and an even greater number thwart the reproductive instinct by observing continence. The determinism of behaviour, then, is not only limited but conditional. While reasons operate according to similar procedures they do not all start from the same premises nor are they directed towards the same ends, the same ideals. The machinery of reason can only work on the material which a particular culture provides: the premises which are started from and the conclusion which is reached may be either rational or irrational, and in the latter case again may be anti-rational or super-rational. A group where the prevailing ideal is to get oneself a grand funeral and an imposing mausoleum will not behave in the same way as a group which aims simply at securing as comfortable a life as possible here and now, or one which is concerned with preparing an earthly or heavenly Jerusalem. The reigning concepts of any group always originate, to a greater or lesser extent, in the mind of a person or persons.

The *determinism of inertia*, finally, is related to certain psychological tendencies inherent in man which lead him to reduce the unknown to the known, the present to the past; it is connected also with the spontaneous conformism which is innate in the group, with the need felt by the person to give his activities an ordered framework of habit, and finally with what the classical economists call the law of least effort. Deep down, it stems from the tendency of every creature to persevere in being as he is. It can be seen operating in the history of ideas, customs and institutions. An idea always springs from a person or from some small group: diffused and therefore simplified, it then becomes a collective representation, a view of the world, which will resist the impact of new conceptions. Similarly, every custom begins with an initial act, comparable to the act whereby a habit is engendered in the person: it develops a life of its own, so to speak, it tends to perpetuate itself, even though it may lose its original meaning. An institution too originates as a freely conceived project in the human will: once set on foot it also tends to take on an independent existence and usually external pressure is necessary before it can be dissolved or even modified.

This determinism too is limited and conditional. The human liberty from which it takes its origin can suspend or annul its effects by reform or innovation, and there are many historical examples of such breaks and continuities. As Joseph Wilbois and Paul Bureau have put it, liberty is like a fresh spring welling forth in successive gushes of water which bubbles out and then spreads in still sheets: these in turn ice over and harden, but beneath its crust of ice the living water flows on, ready to burst out again and to carry the floes of broken ice on towards the sea.

Such is our view of the forms of social determinism: real but limited, relative, conditional and probable, in short, closely corresponding to man's own composite nature.

Social determinism and personal liberty

These conceptions of social determinism involve both theoretical and practical consequences.

It follows firstly that certain "social laws" can be formulated, provided we remember that they are concerned only with averages, that they are valid only in relation to their context, and that their predictions never exceed the realm of probability, at best extreme probability.

Secondly, social determinism not being absolute, human liberty has an effect on society, not only in so far as it modifies physical determinism by bringing nature into subjection at the same time as it obeys it, but in a more direct and fundamental way: society, in fact, is a rational construction of human free will in operation, conditioned of course by geographical environment and historical tradition.

The third consequence is that human liberty of action upon and within society is never absolute but always partially subject to certain socio-psychological conditions. Society is never completely open to the effect of reason, never completely adaptable to free will. All things are neither possible nor even conceivable at all moments and in all places. A social structure is not built on a void, on an absolute vacuum.

At every moment and in every situation we can see determinism and liberty encountering each other, conflicting and collaborating. Their encounter is what constitutes history, and indeed history differs from simple evolution precisely because it is human, it is the result of freedom operating on social determinisms, just as character is the result of free will operating upon natural temperament. This collaboration of free will and determinism is nowhere better illustrated, as Aron and Dardieu have shown, than in the greatest and most effective of historical reforms, the silent revolution in Western Europe between the third and eighth centuries which succeeded in abolishing that essential characteristic of Romano-Hellenistic civilization, the institution of slavery. The work of Lefebvre des Noëttes and Marc Bloch have shown that this revolution was due to two factors, one technical, the other spiritual: firstly it was made possible by the increasing use of horse power for heavy haulage and the replacement of muscular by hydraulic energy, thereby releasing the slaves who had to provide this energy; secondly there was the new Christian message of human dignity and brotherhood which had the effect of making both slaves and masters alike *interiorly* free. Both these processes of liberation, material and spiritual, resulted in an institutional and juridical emancipation, the development of which can be followed in legal history.

Who is responsible for this revolution? Originally it is a matter of individual free choices, but gradually it comes to involve a whole variety of people—unknown inventors, evangelists, masters and slaves, legislators and lawyers.

Key figures

Experience and common sense have made humanity aware of these encounters between free will and determinism. Hence its tenacious preservation of the memory of certain "key figures": great religious leaders such as Buddha, Moses, Mohammed and (prescinding from his divinity) Christ; great thinkers such as Plato, Aristotle or Descartes; great explorers and pioneers such as Christopher Columbus or Magellan; great technicians and inventors such as Stephenson, Pasteur or Fleming, or a simple workman like Jacquard; great statesmen, whether conservative or revolutionary, such as Charlemagne, Richelieu or Lenin; great soldier-politicians such as Alexander or Caesar; heroes or saints like Francis of Assisi and Vincent de Paul—all these have made their mark, the mark of their liberty, on their own time and on our time.

As Carlyle said, this hero cult sometimes attains the dimensions of a myth. Hence the myth of the legislator which in ancient times became attached to half-mythical, half-historical figures like Manon, Lycurgus, Solon, Numa Pompilius and Confucius. And hence, in modern societies, the myth of the great reformer or liberator, exemplified in such figures as Washington, Bolivar, the fathers of the French Revolution or Mustapha Kemal.

These myths, while transfiguring reality, are not pure falsehood. Karl Marx, a man ignored and misunderstood in his own day, was to have an incalculable effect upon history. And what immeasurable consequences the work of a St Vincent de

Paul has had—foreshadowing and initiating all our modern forms of social assistance and social service. One thinks too of Florence Nightingale, the first nurse in the modern sense of the word, who was herself no feminist and yet did more than anyone else to promote the cause of feminism.

Moral obligation

Within society man not only freely determines his own life in accordance with his nature and maintains genuinely personal relations with his fellows, he also acts on social phenomena themselves: forms and structures, representations, customs and mentalities.

The normal, adult man, the man who has attained to the stature of a person, soon learns to distinguish moral obligations from the exterior constraints and interior pressures to which he is subjected by society. Long before Sophocles expressed the truth through the lips of Antigone, man was aware that the positive law of society does not always accord with human law, that sometimes indeed the two may conflict, and that above the written law there is a higher law which is inscribed in man's reason. We have already shown how at the end of infancy a child discovers that the attraction of love, which keeps him close within the family community, cannot be his sole law of action. When the group comes into contact with other groups the conscience becomes aware of conflicting claims, and hence it becomes evident to the person that while the pressure and attraction of the group provide incentives for action they are not sufficient to furnish its motives: it is necessary, in fact, to choose.

Similarly, a gradual distinction is made between strict obligation and the invitation or "call" which comes to the hero or the saint. The latter is something gratuitous, while obligation involves necessity; one tends towards the perfect, the other towards the good; one is a call, the other an order. Man is obliged simply to be a man, but he is called to transcend himself. The whole difference between invitation and obligation is summed up in the well-known remark about great men being more admired than imitated. Obligation has an absolute character—you ought . . . you must . . . it is your duty. The idea of duty implies a debt to be paid, a debt to the nature within one and to all those who share that nature. It also implies obedience, obedience to a set of rules which constitute a law, the moral law, the natural law, and this obedience involves fidelity to what makes me what I am. Obligation, as its etymology indicates, is something binding and I cannot extricate myself from it without renouncing my nature: to refuse obligation is not just to reject an extrinsic imposition but to deny oneself and one's nature; it is a crime against man, a sin, which means a deprivation, a disharmony, the admission of non-being into being.

Obligation, as an absolute, must itself be based upon an absolute. Now man's personal nature is not an absolute, nor his social nature and the group it creates, nor nature envisaged universally. These are all contingent and relative: they may provide the proximate preparation for obligation but they cannot be its ultimate foundation, any more than they can provide the ultimate end for action. The truth will out in the end; to apotheosize what is merely relative and contingent however specious it may seem is to be guilty of idolatry, to bow the knee to Moloch. Fellowship, the sense of community, however strong, is a social phenomenon and not a social law. Obviously I have debts towards my fellows, but who tells me I must pay my debts? To quote the famous saying, that is a notion put about by bank managers. Absolute moral obligation can only be based on the true absolute, the eternal and infinite God who creates and preserves my nature and endows it with essence and existence, and who is my supreme end, the fulfilment of my destiny and the goal of my journey. It is the divine law which guarantees the natural law, which in turn guarantees the positive law: the temporal is dependent on the eternal. This divine law is no arbitrary and extrinsic precept accompanied by juridical sanctions but something intrinsic to the nature and person of every man, bound up with and yet transcending them, just as God present within me can fulfil my nature more truly than I can myself. If there are sanctions, they are within the person himself: either he fulfils himself or decays, either he succeeds or fails in the pursuit of his eternal destiny.

Social morality, then, as much as personal morality, is founded upon the divine Absolute, because it is God who created man's social nature. The divine Absolute is the link which makes social obligation firm and maintains the cohesion of men in association; it is the sovereign Good towards which societies and the persons who compose them tend; it is the supreme authority whence all social authorities derive their jurisdiction and the supreme liberty of which all other liberties are a reflection. . . . Without him societies founder, lacking purpose and order, social relations are dissolved in the flux of relativity, social ties become illusory or oppressive, social activity becomes a tyranny and liberty disintegrates into anarchy, the world is left to the mercy of force and chance like a condemned man thrown to the beasts, and history becomes no more than a wild tale told by a fool.

As we showed at the beginning of the chapter, the realization of absolute obligation comes to man through the contemplation of his own free, rational and therefore responsible and moral nature which is a social nature and a spiritual nature, susceptible of God and tending towards God.

Man is a rational animal, and as such he rationalizes everything about him, including nature and society. He is also a creature made in the image of God and as such he cannot help imparting divinity to everything with which he comes into contact, from the mere fact that he makes them human.

Man is led to the same discoveries and comes to realize the social implications of moral obligation by the interior dialectic of his activity. On the one hand, experience teaches him that his personal fulfilment is dependent on social conditions. He cannot act as a man unless he attains that minimum of well-being which is necessary for the life of the spirit, without that minimum of security which is necessary for contemplation, without social order. Again, experience shows him that he is able to change social conditions and impose an order upon them, provisionally at least. This conception of an order presupposes a general view of man and society which in turn implies a vision of the cosmic order, for every social order reflects what men see as the order of the universe. At the centre of this order there must be a keystone, an absolute, and this, if it is to be, must be divine.

From another point of view we may argue as follows: man acts, simply because he must act in order to live. As a social animal he must engage in social activity because his individual action needs the force of common action if it is to increase and multiply, and also because it is always situated in a social context. As a rational animal he cannot be content with action as such, action for its own sake: even the most activist of men must needs reflect, must enquire into the Why as well as the How of their acts. Indeed the very question of the How of their acts will present them with certain questions: as manufacture depends on technical rules, so action demands rules of action. In his pursuit of ends man must eventually seek for a supreme end, unless he is to go round in a circle like a traveller lost in a forest or indefinitely to follow a straight line; there comes a moment when he must achieve an ultimate transition which transcends what has gone before, to the final end which is at the same time the first end. Proceeding from proximate to ultimate rules he will finally attain that first axiom which contains all the others in potency and he will have to estimate the authority of this fundamental principle which can only be based upon the absolute.

Finally, similar questions and answers are to be found in history itself, that result of determinism and liberty in collaboration. Does history have a meaning? If it does, if for instance through its various detours and vicissitudes it follows a certain law of progress, it is clear that it derives this meaning from human liberty, since it is a human phenomenon. In what direction should men guide history? Does not history have its end in that very God who also initiated it in creating the universe? History, in fact, is a return to God by a progressive humanization of nature and divinization of humanity, a process which involves no confusion in the distinction between creature and Creator.

All roads lead to the Absolute, all roads start from the Absolute. God is the principle of moral obligation in society, as he is the principle of nature and society themselves. He guarantees the social order, as he guarantees the order of the universe and the interior human order.

Social moralism

As all moral obligation is based on the same obligation, so this action can be seen as one single process of humanization which varies according to the different realities it affects. We must not think of personal morality and social morality as twin systems proceeding from one obligation, but rather of one single morality which wears different aspects and involves different obligations. In the same way, there is not one morality of pure obligation and another morality of pure aspiration, each separated from the other; obligation and aspiration, precept and counsel, though distinct and unconfused, correlate and complement each other; the call of the hero or the saint presupposes but goes beyond the prescriptions of the legislator. Morality, even what theologians call natural morality, involves the law of love (we are not of course concerned here with the theological virtue of charity) and hence obligation cannot be independent of aspiration.

This whole dynamic moral impetus explains the twofold aspect of social morality. On the one hand, it may be regarded as governing the behaviour of the person in the group and towards the group, laying down the moral conduct he should follow in the situation with which he is presented. How for instance in a capitalist business will employer and employees conduct themselves in accordance with justice? This morality cannot but seem static and casuistical, though it is necessary nevertheless, for we have to live fully as men here and now. To confine oneself to it, however, would be an impoverishment of social morality, which also governs the action of man *upon* the group, the humanization of the group by the constant reform of institutions and habits. This social activity springs from a dissatisfaction caused by the difficulty or impossibility of fulfilling one's obligations in a given context or else bred by higher aspirations. This latter morality is no less dynamic than the former.

Here, as throughout the preceding argument, we are diametrically opposed to that inflated form of morality which we call moralism.

Moralism may consist in reducing social morality to its consequences for personal behaviour. On this view man simply contents himself with fulfilling his social duties and "giving a good example" in whatever his situation happens to be: he never questions his conditions, he accepts them, never attempting to give them a new orientation; he lives in the present, and leaves the future to itself. This attitude, the occupational temptation of every established class, really means another victory for individualism. When it becomes hard and fast it can inculcate a self-satisfied Pharisaism, an "I'm all right Jack" kind of conscience.

There is another moralism, diametrically opposed to this, which is the temptation of less privileged classes which are liable to resentment. It is characterized by a complete and absolute condemnation of the present delivered in the name of morality: everything is corrupt, there must be a new beginning, which can only be effected by a catastrophe, a day of reckoning or judgement. Meanwhile there is no point in attempting anything, since every effort would be in vain, or so far short of the ideal striven for, so tainted by the present corruption that it would only sully the hands and hearts of those who are in any case simply patching up a building which is doomed to destruction. It is for man to let the process of decay go forward, even helping it on if need be. This cataclysmic moralism also tends to produce a Pharisaical attitude.

Moralism can also take the form of the impersonal statement of moral truths—one remembers the untimely pulpit oratory of the preacher derided in Albert Camus' novel *The Plague*—or of the rigid application of a general rule to particular situations which is much more dangerous. There is the moralism which makes a facile combination of general principles in order to produce an automatic solution for a particular case, and there is the intrusion of morality, which is a normative science, into the social sciences. In every case moralism has the effect of making social morality something marginal and inessential—what Nietzsche called an injection of moraline.

But social morality as we have defined it is not extrinsic to social realities since it stems from the very nature of man and of society; it is not just an outward adornment of these realities, it is central to them and responds to their deepest needs. Doubtless it is rash to claim to discover moral laws in social life by empirical observation, like Frédéric Le Play with the Ten Commandments. Such a conclusion would be an inadmissible substitution of the normative for the positive. Observation certainly shows that all societies recognize a morality and that these various moralities contain general if not universal constants which correspond to the terms of natural law. Historical moralities are relative, it is true, but we must not exaggerate their relativity; there are few known groups which regard it as moral to eat or even to abandon one's old parents or children, at least as a common rule. The purely arbitrary prohibitions and injunctions embodied in these moralities are eventually eliminated, as for instance the taboos of exogamy or endogamy which once prevailed in totemic clan societies have long since disappeared.

Between moral life and social life, between moral action and social action there is not an artificial opposition, which gives rise to moralism or immoralism, but a correspondence that reflects the unity of the human spirit. Similarly, there can be no contradiction between the normative science of morality and the social sciences so long as the latter remain faithful to their task, which is to describe society as it is, not as it ought to be. In the past the social sciences have been regarded as ancillaries or even simply as aspects of ethics, but the methodological advances which have given the human sciences an autonomy corresponding to their particular formal objects now forbid any such appropriation. But differences in object and method do not mean opposition, and the social arts, which are derived from the social sciences, remain subaltern to morality which is the science of human action.

As for the application of moral principles to social situations for the purpose of immediate and concrete action, this cannot be quasi-automatic even by a subtle combination of diverse imperatives; the rule is general, while the case is particular, and so application of the general rule to the particular case is what the scholastics called "speculativo-practical". Abrupt and hasty application of a general rule can defeat its own purpose, either because it turns out to be ineffectual or because it involves errors of adjustment which further complicate an already complex situation. Similarly while the casuistical combination of principles can solve certain problems, particularly those of a juridical character, like the problem of restitution, it cannot claim to provide automatic and infallible solutions. Not that the situation abolishes the rule—this would be adopting Situation Ethics and the subjectivist position—nor does it mean that casuistry is simply an irrelevant frivolity. It means that moral action in a given context must involve the personal exercise of the virtue of prudence which makes its practical judgement in accordance with the principles and the situation alike. This view avoids both moralism and immoralism. In certain extreme cases, which are the deadly consequence of collective sin, practically no adequate solution can in fact be found short of heroism, which in the ordinary way cannot be demanded of the majority of men. Consequently, moral duty consists in doing what little one can, as best one can, while not resting content with this minimum, that is to say recognizing one's impotence with clear-sighted humility and trying to improve the situation, if necessary by making common cause with those who are victims of the same circumstances. This is, for example the position of an employer who is prevented by economic and social conditions from providing a just wage.

Moral action is not to be confused with practical and immediate effectiveness, although ordinarily at least the latter goes with it. An ineffectual morality, a morality "with no hands"—to use Péguy's phrase—would not be a human morality and Ruskin's saying: The most beautiful things in the world are the most useless, betrays an outlook confined to literary men or Stoics. Sisyphus, rolling his stone up the mountain, could not keep up his courage unless he retained some hope of reaching the top, or at least some level on the way; and the labour of Penelope, weaving, unweaving and re-weaving her cloth, would be pointless were she not waiting for Ulysses—which is not the same as waiting for Godot. The fact that a human morality "has hands" means that these hands are liable to get soiled and dirty: man as a moral and social creature has to come to terms with harsh reality, he has to be content for a time with compromises, half-measures and half-successes, and sometimes he will have to make a leap in the dark, when he can see no further than his own conscience. A human morality must be applied and so must become incarnate—with all the limitations, the adulteration, and the risks that incarnation involves. This is a far cry from the moralist position, but the essential error of moralism is precisely the fact that it brings discredit on morality by making it seem ineffectual, thus adding grist to the mill of the immoralists.

Obligations, their unity and analogy

Moralism can produce a certain rigidity, a certain univocity in the ideas and applications of social morality: it tends to transfer the rules which govern interpersonal relations, without any modification, into the sphere of social relations.

It was Benedict XV who reminded us during the First World War that there cannot be two moralities, one for the individual and the other for society, and this idea of a double morality is one which we have set ourselves to refute. Morality is a single whole, one and the same commandment, and the obligation to love one's neighbour is not confined to one's particular class or nation. To limit morality in this way is to create an interior contradiction which will destroy it; this was the error of the German jurist Carl Schmidt who while claiming to be applying the morality of the Gospel made a distinction between the private enemy, whom one must love, and the public enemy whom one may hate.

While obligation remains always and everywhere the same there is a graded scale of obligations corresponding to personal situations. My neighbour is indeed every man but as the term neighbour implies, he is first of all the man who is nearest to me, the man next door. Common sense will tell us that our more immediate and pressing obligations are towards the individuals and groups with which we have actual contact. It is not very hard to love the Papuans or Patagonians, but it is asking something real of me here and now to love my wife, my children or even my mother-in-law. It is good to love humanity—not just as an abstraction but as a community in process of growth—but for most of the time I can only prove this love by loving that section of humanity in which I am historically and geographically situated. Again, while I must have a care for future generations I must not thereby forget the present generation. It is evident that this awareness of a scale of obligations and the immediacy of the obligations due to those who are nearest me have certain consequences for social morality, for the closer the spheres of social and interpersonal action become the more completely does social obligation resemble interpersonal obligation.

Moreover, while moral precepts are the same, they are applied analogically to their various objects. One cannot expect groups or the authorities which represent them to behave in exactly the same way as persons: one must take account of the importance of the interests involved in common ownership, or simply of the unwieldiness which is inevitable in any collectivity. Here again common sense has its suggestions. While a person may accept risks for which he alone will take the consequences, common charity forbids him to impose these risks on the group for which he is responsible. Individually he can make heroic choices of which the group is incapable. It is hardly necessary to say that a person may totally abstain from alcohol, either for an ascetical purpose or to set an example or simply for the sake of health. But experience shows that when such abstinence is enforced on large groups of people, disastrous consequences can ensue. Again, personal homicide, except in the case of legitimate self-defence, is always immoral, but the juridical death penalty or collective homicide in the time of war are not immoral, even though they may not exactly represent the peak of moral perfection; if they intend more than a mere pious aspiration, those who advocate summary abolition are in danger of creating worse evils than those they are intending to remedy. This does not mean, of course, that one should not strive for the suppression of these forms of killing, certainly for the abolition of the horror of war—the death penalty poses more complex problems. In its excessive preoccupation with morality and perfection social moralism sometimes leads only to a redoubting of immorality, just as the perfectionism of some parents can have an adverse effect on their children. Morality is a single whole, while its applications are analogous—a fact which undeniably leads to tension between the person and the social body, especially when the two are at variance in their morality. These outward tensions are, after all, no more than the expression of an inward tension, the tension of the person divided between his personal and his social being.

"Open" and "closed" societies

This tension is exacerbated, and sometimes turned into a conflict by that gravitational pull which is natural to the group and which we showed above to be the effect of social conformism and the determinism of inertia. No one has thrown more light on this problem than Bergson, who originated the distinction between the "open" and the "closed" society.

Social bodies, which are relational beings, do not possess an awareness of moral obligation nor a rule of morality, but their determining influence affects the consciences and actions of persons who are moral beings. Every society of itself tends to become closed, that is to say it tends to demand conformity from its members, a conformity which goes beyond the loyalties which are a normal adjunct of belonging to any society: it tends to remain in the *status quo*, or rather to evolve only under the pressure of external determinism and to adopt an exclusive attitude towards other groups. The closed society does not refuse to expand but it envisages expansion primarily as supplanting or absorbing other groups. Closedness in fact is not so much a geographical or strictly social phenomenon as a psychological one; even a universal society could be a closed society if it were to claim self-sufficiency and deny a transcendent power. Thus society has a tendency towards self-sufficiency, totalitarianism and imperialism, a tendency to demand an exclusive and total allegiance, and social conformism can lead man to a theoretical or practical sociolatry, to the worship of the group. These tendencies can be seen even in religious societies, where they take the form of sectarianism or clericalism.

By the pressure which they exert on persons closed societies tend to develop their own closed morality, often with an attendant ideology and mythology. These moralities impose themselves upon individuals from without, even where they appear to be intrinsic, and they warp consciences that are corrupted by collective representations and moral conformism. It is this coerciveness and this rejection of universality which are their chief characteristics, for any obligations they may involve in theory or practice are only obligations within and towards the group. Hence the inevitable arbitrariness of these obligations, which exist simply to satisfy the passing needs of the group or the current trend of behaviour. The average end-product of such a morality is the "well-ordered conscience". An open morality, on the other hand, is essentially interior, universal in its principles, rational and reasonable, always ready to welcome inspiration; it produces not the self-satisfaction of the "good conscience" but a spirit of restlessness, and it aims not at mass-producing average individuals but at bringing forth saints and heroes.

When we said earlier that there are correspondences between moral life and social life we were right in so far as social life is truly human, but we should add the qualification that society can allow itself to be completely determined. Correspondences do not mean that there are no conflicts.

The distinction between the closed society and the open society is not a dichotomy; in fact, any one society contains elements of each, inextricably mingled. The action of personal liberty and the intervention of heroes and saints keep social bodies from closing up finally and completely, and even the clashes and struggles of groups have the effect of opening them up to each other. On the other hand, the closed morality does tend to debase an open morality, which it adapts to the interests or ideas of the group. The coexistence of the closed and the open society is reflected in the history of law. Law always tends to ratify a closed morality, but the pressure of new facts and the action of reformers force it to make constant modifications.

The opening up of a society is done by persons, or by small groups in which interpersonal relations prevail. When one speaks of political and social liberties one does not mean the liberty of the groups themselves so much as the liberty of persons as affected by and in the group. Juridical, individual or collective liberties make possible the exercise of psychological and moral liberties. This development is assisted by the fact that the person belongs to a number of groups at once, as Dürkheim and Bouglé noted. The man who belongs to one group only tends always to be its creature. It is in the areas where groups connect and where they are opposed that liberty is to be found. Innovation, reform, social progress—all these things in the first and last resort stem from *personal* initiative, thought or action, even though the person never acts in isolation but always operates within a particular social context, in collaboration or conflict with other persons and groups. Here again is that vital encounter between determinism and liberty, between person and society. Societies tend to become closed, and persons, using the means society offers, open them up again.

Commitment

The struggle of the person to maintain the existence of the group and to prevent it from becoming closed, the conscious, free and active acceptance of a social situation, together with the responsibilities and fellowship it entails—this is what we call personal commitment, which is not to be confused with any kind of dragooning or press-ganging. The mother or housewife who accepts her state of life, freely adhering to the portion nature has allotted her, is far more truly committed than the political militants who are always ready to climb off their bandwagon. In one sense the person is always committed, whether he likes it or not, in virtue of his situation, but to deserve its name this commitment must have his signature and approval.

By his self-commitment the person realizes his vocation: what begins as necessity is transformed into a human destiny. He gives himself to his fellow men, but in the way that a person gives himself—not surrendering what makes him a person. He belongs to the group in order to play a full part in it, that is to say not just a passive but an active part. His activity goes to maintain the being of the group, defending it if necessary even by the use of force, and the life of the group, which is a process of movement and change—not a vague, undirected movement but a movement towards the ends imposed by the never-ending needs of the open morality. Within the group he bears witness to freedom by collaboration as well as by conflict, and by his joyful readiness to meet obligations and calls he opens the group up and furthers its progress. He makes it more open in order that the human and the divine may fill it more completely. In actual practice he works by making foundations when new organisms or new institutions appear necessary or by imbuing a new spirit when it is simply a matter of improving existing structures or purifying or reviving group representations. Self-commitment is always a leap in the dark: the consequences of one's self-commitment can be more far-reaching than one expects, or even quite different.

Fifty years ago, a young Grenoble engineer called Émile Romanet was so moved by the conditions of working-class families that he decided to dedicate himself to improving their lot and invented a system of family allowances provided by compensation funds. Probably he had no idea that he was paving the way for a renewal of French family life.

Francis of Assisi by rebuilding a ruined church began a process which ended with the restoration of the Church itself. Again, Ignatius of Loyola, the man who had to give up his longed-for pilgrimage to Jerusalem, was to give the decisive impetus to the Counter-Reformation.

For the person

If the person gives society this orientation it is because he acts for all other persons with that purpose which has become the motto of Protestant socialism—in order that every man, the whole of man and all mankind may grow to their full stature and effect a transfiguration of nature in an all-inclusive return to the personal God.

The ultimate aim and purpose of society is in fact that every person may be realized in the image of God. Relational being cannot find its end in itself, only in a subsistent being, which is the basis for relations. Because it is relational, it is essentially *ad alterum*, directed towards another, and this other must be a person, itself directed towards God. To commit the error of sociolatry is not only to cheat God by misappropriating the adoration due to him alone, but to cheat man by despoiling him and imprisoning his personal being within the confines of what is merely relative. It is this which constitutes the alienation of man: the ravages wrought on man by capitalism are only one of the innumerable forms which this alienation takes. The exploitation of man by man, which is hateful when practised by individual on individual is perhaps even more hateful when practised by society on the person. Man is not a commodity to be exploited, a tool to be made use of, a form of capital to be administered: he is a man, the greatest of all created beings. Man and society belong to different orders, for the former belongs to a superior order of imperishable spirits, while the latter is perishable. Society is connatural with time, while the person is connatural with both time and eternity. Within the scale of final causes, the lower end must further the higher end: hence, any group which stifles individual self-fulfilment instead of assisting it, which shackles man instead of setting him free, is failing in its purpose and betraying its function.

Are we then to return to anarchic or liberal individualism? The answer is No. We are concerned here with the person as such, not with the individual. The distinction between person and individual must not indeed be abused, for it is only a distinction of reason, based on reality. To attempt to solve all conflicts between person and society by recourse to it would be to offer merely notional or verbal solutions. Yet the distinction remains a valid one: the end of society is not the material satisfaction of individuals, which is no more than a means, nor the aggrandisement of their egos, nor the satisfaction of their various desires, some of which may be wrong or disordered, nor even the development of their personalities, which is the separate concern of each and must involve respect for other personalities. The end of society is the full growth of what constitutes the individual as a person, in other words, his reason and liberty, and the realization of his personal vocation, whereby he answers God's call in a situation which he at once accepts and fashions.

Man himself, who is thus led to the goal of his journey, is a social being, whose destiny is knit with the destiny of the communities and societies in which he finds himself. He realizes his destiny only in realizing theirs, and they realize theirs only by realizing his. The vocation of the person is therefore obviously inseparable from the acceptance of social and communal ties, together with the discipline and sacrifices they entail. The person cannot exist, cannot persist, without society; he must also pay society a price for services rendered, in the form of copyright, passport and residence permit. Society is not a game which one gives up when it ceases to amuse and whose rules one alters at one's convenience, nor is it a group of children collected and disbanded according to whim. It demands the self-commitment of responsible adults or of the young people it leads to adulthood. The adult knows how to accept discipline, while the young are apprenticed to its acceptance by its enforcement. In the order of final causes the person is prior, but in the order of action (the distinction is Jacques Maritain's) he is subordinate to society and its authorities. This subordination is a logical consequence of the fact that society is a relational being, since relation orders subsistent beings not *for* each other but in relation *to* each other, in accordance with their end and in accordance with a whole pattern of relations. By the activities which follow from his relations, the person also has his part in this whole pattern. To deny this would be to deviate from personalism into individualism. Mounier, the founder of the personalist movement, showed his awareness of this in his refusal to separate the personal from the communal.

This twofold and opposing hierarchy of ends and action which makes persons and societies reciprocally subordinate can be seen in operation when we come to consider the common good of the group.

Through the common good

Like all goods the common good is an object desired by the will because in so far as it is good it corresponds to the aspiration of being towards self-fulfilment. It fulfils personal being and social being at the same time.

The common good must not be confused with the general interest. Interests involve limitations and conflicts, and the word general implies opposition to the particular. The common good is not, at least in the nature of things, opposed to the particular good, but rather it conditions, assumes and contains it. It does not soar in some empyrean far above the particular good: it both transcends and embraces it.

The common good may be described, rather than defined, as the whole complex of wealth, resources, institutions, representations, behaviour and projects in which the members of a group all share, actively and passively, as givers and takers. The goods which go to make up the common good are of every kind; some, like wealth and technology, are purely material and useful; others, like institutions, are relational but still confined to the sphere of utility; others are spiritual and invested with the dignity of intermediate ends, such as truth, justice and peace; others again, like culture, literature and the arts, mark the point of encounter between useful and spiritual, means and ends. A scale is established between these goods which accords with their nature and at the same time with the ends pursued by society. Thus of its very nature the common good is hierarchical and organic. It is also dynamic, situated in the present but heir to the past and looking forward to the future, within the continuity and movement of succeeding generations. One cannot be content merely with preserving or safeguarding the common good; it must be secured by well-laid designs.

Every group has its common good, whose parts are arranged in relation to its ends. When one group is integrated into another larger group, above all into the universal society, its own good becomes a particular good in relation to the good of the whole. So it is right up the scale from the smallest of all societies, the family, to the human community itself. The requirements of the common good form the basis for the system of relations obtaining within each group and between different groups, and also for the rights of the authorities who are responsible for these relations and the common good.

There is a distinction but no essential opposition between the common good and the particular goods of persons or groups. The common good of humanity includes the good of the persons who go to make up the various human groups, and consequently in a universal society it includes the good of the groups which are necessary for the good of the person. The fulfilment of a particular man's personality does no disservice to the common good; on the contrary, it helps to enrich it; in return, that man will work all the more ardently for the common good, seeing that it is the indispensable condition of his fulfilment.

In fact, however, certain incompatibilities arise which can develop into open conflict. These stem from the contingency and inevitable limitation which attend personal and social action, from intellectual error and moral inadequacy. They point to the imperfection of a world where men must fulfil their nature without ever being able to attain complete success, where persons and institutions tend to corrupt each other, where the forces of determinism can be seen and grappled with but never destroyed. Sometimes the restrictions demanded by the common good become insupportable to the person so that the person rejects or evades them, to the detriment of his own and the common good. Tension is never absent from society because it is the interior law of the person. Even in the perfectly integrated group, in a period of tranquillity, man never fully attains a feeling of happiness.

Where conflict does arise the common good must win on balance, because its extension is wider than that of particular goods and affects a greater number of persons, because it provides the very conditions for particular goods, and finally because it has something "divine" about it, to use St Thomas's term, *aliquid divinum*. The authorities who are responsible for it are entitled therefore to demand from persons the sacrifices which it necessarily entails, even, it may be, the sacrifice of life itself, although of course they may never require the person to abdicate his dignity, reason or liberty or to perform an intrinsically inhuman act, a criminal act for instance, which would make him forfeit his status as a person.

This submission of the person to the common good and this orientation of the common good towards the person is what constitutes the social order.

In justice and love

The social order of man goes by the name of *justice*. Justice renders to each, whether it be a person or a society, his due, in accordance with the general principles of law, in conformity with the natural law and hence with the divine law. It pays the debts owed by the person to other persons and societies, and the debts owned by societies to other societies. It transfigures and humanizes the whole system of relations which constitutes a society, bestowing on them a legal status and causing them to proceed according to the rules of law. Basically social morality consists to a great extent in the application of justice to situations which are based on the varying types of social relations, and to these situations themselves. There is domestic justice, economic justice, civic justice, cultural justice—a justice for all relations and situations.

Justice is marked by objectivity, universality and the rigorous character of the obligations it imposes. It pronounces its judgements in accordance with certain rules, not allowing itself to be swayed by instincts or particular interests. It views all persons and groups impartially; if it must make special allowances, as in the case of distributive justice, it always does so in accordance with certain objective general rules, irrespective of any sympathies or antipathies. Its judgements may be slightly adapted, they may be open to different interpretations and in case of doubt may result in several possibilities but they are always deliberate and they must always be carried out.

That is why, in spite of what is often said nowadays, justice by itself does not constitute an adequate foundation for social peace, still less for communal order in groups like the family or nation. For that we also need equity which can extend or modify the law as need arises in order to prevent pure legal theory turning into injustice; there is a need too for the dispositions which Taparelli d'Azeglio has called goodwill and beneficence, which proceed from man's social nature and from his natural gifts of sympathy; we need what the Greeks called civic friendship; to go still further, we need love, or to use the Christian term, charity. But without order, peace is merely illusory, and without justice social order is not truly human.

To emphasize love to the detriment of justice is a dangerous mistake. The law of love is its very spontaneity. Love on its own without justice leaves the world at the mercy of the irrational and its freedom degenerates into mere caprice: deprived of the support and protection which law assures it, it withers away or turns into hatred. To exalt love at the expense of law is always the temptation of emotional and, if I may say so, feminine minds. Proudhon, with those resources of commonsense inherited from his peasant forefathers, was right to assail it. It is an equally dangerous mistake to submit love to law, as socialism does. Law provides only a partial satisfaction of the person's needs, for as a creature capable of love he wants also to be loved. Without love, justice tends to harden the arteries of social life, to desiccate it—and to its own detriment, for one can only render true justice to those one loves. This error is the temptation of rigorous and more masculine minds, but it remains a temptation.

Love not only perfects justice, it penetrates, inspires and animates it from within. Its aspirations prevent justice from becoming self-sufficient, from being imprisoned in its own formulas, from yielding to pressure from closed moralities.

Justice and law owe their continued evolution to the beckonings and impulses and very distractions of love. It begins with the scales of Themis, with the material or mathematical equality of commutative justice, the justice which governs exchanges, or of the *lex talionis* which is a form of penal exchange. Little by little this concept of equality is developed and modified as the forms of justice become diversified. Mankind has seen the advent of distributive justice, the justice of governing authority which treats its subjects according to their powers, abilities, deserts and needs, within a complex of relations and situations; social justice, which associates the person with the common good of the group by moral and juridical obligations; penal justice which seeks not just to punish the offender in order to repair the damage done to the social order but also to reform and to rehabilitate him; international justice which governs the relations between peoples and nations.

In our own day the problems presented by the under-developed countries have given rise to a further development still, that of international social justice. In the progress of penal law from its origins in the *lex talionis*, ordeal, vendetta and wehrgeld, and in the progress of social law up to the point when at the beginning of the nineteenth century a law could be passed controlling the employment of juveniles, we can see justice evolving under the inspiration of love, a love embodied in heroes and saints or in ordinary persons striving to lead a better life in order to bring others to do the same. By evolving, justice does not cease to be itself but it lives and develops. Ontologically and psychologically justice and love will remain distinct. Often, however, the charity of today becomes the justice of tomorrow. The gentle constraint of love's call keeps justice up to the mark in following its own path of progress and fulfilment.

Towards progress

Love and justice, therefore, follow inevitably a law of progress which is at the same time the law of persons and societies, the law of life, the law of the spirit. A person who does not progress in the spiritual life lapses into tepidity, which means regression. Similarly, a society which does not advance becomes stagnant, and stagnation is the prelude to decay and death. When they no longer strive towards progress, justice and love are close to corruption.

By progress here we do not mean material and technical progress. This is an over-simplification of our own times. We do not distrust material progress; on the contrary, we value it in its own order as a good. Its meaning and value ultimately depend on whether or not man uses it in the service of his fellow men, but it does involve a basic ambiguity. One cannot forget Hiroshima.

Nor do we mean by progress that automatic, rectilinear and uninterrupted movement idealized by the Enlightenment. This kind of progress ceases as soon as evolution emerges into history, that is to say, with the advent of man, with his powers of freedom and choice, tragedy and drama. Man gives a meaning to the evolution which has preceded him but at the same time as he perfects this evolution his powers of freedom for the first time break its continuity.

Nor are we concerned here with pure movement regarded in isolation independently of its first and last terms. Change does not necessarily mean progress. Movement is the law of life but it is not its own law. Humanly it is meaningless unless it measures an advance towards a definite objective.

Social progress is human progress, allowing man to grow to his full human stature, growing ever stronger in soul and in body, more completely rational and free, more of a person, more integrated into society, growing in nature and grace and being gradually transformed into that image of God which is already imprinted on his nature. Personal progress and social progress are as inseparable as personal man and social man. The ideal of Progress is not the progressive absorption of the Person by a political Leviathan mistaken for Mankind, nor the complete liberty of individuals in an idyllic and anarchic Eden designed on the lines of a nudist colony; its ideal is that of strong personalities bound by strong ties to strong societies. It is not a vast monody nor a cacophony but a harmony in which diversity goes to create unity in a counter-point which culminates in the final chord.

What form will this harmony take? Reason cannot tell us: we must use the eyes of faith. Meanwhile social progress is obviously neither continual nor infallible. It advances and recoils, it includes mill-races and cataracts, dramas and catastrophes, dialectics of life and dialectics of death. It is not achieved by any automatic synthesis but by weighing the successive claims of justice, involving tension, sacrifice and suffering. We progress when we have climbed a step on our journey but hardly have we done so when, if we are not to sink back, we must start climbing again, without even time for drawing breath. And, since we are free, there is always the possibility of failure. History is a process of development or decay.

It is from moral action, then, that the societies and civilizations which go to make up the human caravan get their direction. We must now find out whether it finds its goal on this earth or whether the law of Transcendence which governs its progress does not lead it beyond earth and time.

CHAPTER III

CONCLUSION: BEYOND SOCIETY

The brief final section of our thesis is in the nature of a transition, the final stage whereby social life is consummated in spiritual life and human time is transcended in divine eternity. We enter into the realm of social theology, a science which is not to be identified with pure metaphysics nor even with natural morality and natural law, but which is concerned with establishing what our concepts of society and man's place in it owe to the Gospel, and which in the light of Revelation examines the part played by the social phenomenon in the human context and the part played by man in God's plan.

The divine society

Theological thought revolves around three basic dogmas, the Trinity, the Incarnation and the Redemption. As P. de Lubac has shown, all dogmas, and particularly these three, involve consequences for society.

The Trinity is a divine society, three persons in one nature. This society which is in God, which is God's, is clearly reflected in our own human societies for which it is a pattern and ideal. The Father begets the Son, and the Holy Spirit proceeds from the Father and the Son, being their mutual love: thus the being of each Person is constituted by a relation within the divine Unity. There are not three Gods, nor one unitary and solitary

God, but rather a divine society of three Persons, persons in the full sense of the term, who are relations of love in the one God, the God who is subsistent Love.

This puts an entirely new light on our conception of the human person. Created in the image of the personal God, the person reflects the divine model by the relations which operate within its unity between its diverse faculties of intelligence, affectivity and will. We can see an individual personal vocation for what it is, not just the working out of a destiny that is at once free and determined, but a process of gradual conformation with God which starts with the initial conditions given by nature and culminates in a transforming union with the divine: it is a personal response to a supremely and mysteriously personal God, a continual progress of love responding to the unceasing invitation of Love himself.

The human person then must become conformed to the personal God. So also human relations within societies, which are relational systems, are gradually conformed to the divine relations and become relations of love based on diversity and unity—diversity of persons and unity of the social body. They are the means whereby the person may develop his body and soul, but they are also the occasions of Love: the human person becomes more like the personal God the better he imitates him and the more effective and coherent his action becomes.

Only love, therefore, can make the social bond strong and lasting. Love is the foundation of society, which does not, of course, mean that it can do without justice, though it can go further than justice and realizes its full possibilities. It follows also that the social authorities in their turn must in their government of society take their example from the divine society, that is to say they must permeate the relations for which they are responsible with the spirit of love, so that these social bonds may not be obstacles to love but rather occasions for men to love one another. Since they derive their authority from God, through the intermediary of social nature and the common good, they must imitate him who both grants and guarantees their function. They cannot declare their independence of God and turn away from him without fatal contradiction. If they claim to love only themselves and present themselves as the fit end of their subjects' love then they fall into idolatry. The obligation of love is all the more pressing, therefore, on those who have charge of communities, which are founded on love and hence should bring about the flowering of love; the father of a family, for instance, must imitate in his own fatherhood the divine Fatherhood from which it takes its origin.

These suggestions indicate the intrinsic dignity of authority which is a mission of love in the service of men.

The law of Incarnation

The second person of the divine society, the Word, became incarnate in order to make man divine, in order to give human history its full meaning, by the movement which leads it from the Creation to that Last Judgement when humanity will pass judgement on itself under the scrutiny of Justice itself. What social lessons are we to derive from this dogma?

First of all we should gain an added respect for the human person, from the fact that one of the three divine Persons thought fit to devoid himself—*exinanivit semetipsum*, as St Paul says—in order to guarantee our condition, including its humblest necessities, and our life.

The Old Testament says that God placed man a little below the angels. The Incarnation reverses this order to some extent in giving man a privilege which is denied to the angels. Hence it gives a new meaning to the vocation of man: man is called not merely to fulfil himself as a man but to become divine, an adopted son of God in the brotherhood of Christ. For Christ as the Word is the First-Born, the efficient and final cause of history, and as Man he is the fully perfect and adult human being who realizes all the spiritual potentialities of human nature.

The Incarnation gives history its meaning and man's pilgrimage its final goal. Humanity proceeded from God, who created it and maintains it in being, and it returns to its Creator by that slow and gradual ascent which is true history—not the history of historians but the history which the angels record. Step by step humanity wends its way towards its final goal, guided by a divine pedagogy, made manifest by the Incarnation which began with the Old Testament theophanies and looks forward to the consummation of time. Thus the meaning of history is gradually revealed, for human societies make their contribution to history through the interaction of persons and societies, by means of institutions as well as events. Mankind advances from event to event, proceeding towards the divine Parousia. Though no earthly society may claim to be an abiding dwelling place, and though man, the pilgrim, can have no true kingdom here below, since his own fatherland can never be one with the kingdom of the divine Father, yet societies gain a new dimension from the Incarnation: they are more than mere lodging-houses on man's road. The fact that human fatherhood reflects the fatherhood of God reveals the true dignity of our earthly fatherlands. Man, the pilgrim, cannot adopt a false attitude of detachment towards the dwellings he builds on his journey, nor can he treat them with scorn or negligence, for they are a normal consequence of the fact that his nature, like Christ's, is incarnate in time and history and thus they deserve the respect which is due to human nature and which Christ himself showed by his deference to authority and also by his love for his people and his native land.

As an incarnate spirit, just as Christ is incarnate God, man is subject to the law of the Incarnation: he must make his imprint on the things of nature, rendering them divine precisely by making them human, in order to free the creature which yearns to return to its Creator. While living in time and accepting its necessities, he must permeate it with the divine and turn it towards eternity. He must regard his body not with resignation but with joy, treating it as his good servant. Finally, he must abandon society to the play of determinism, he must set it free, permeating it too with justice and love and directing it towards God, its final end. If the evolution of the world has any meaning, which it must, then it represents a progression from the material to the organic, from the organic towards the animal and from the animal towards man: man culminates the Creation because he can know it from the inside and act upon it in order to make it human, in the way that Adam cultivated the garden of Eden. At this stage God intervenes and the movement towards humanization becomes a movement towards divinization. Human liberty which is a reflection of divine liberty leaves its mark on the world by making history. To quote Teilhard de Chardin, the biosphere gives place to the noosphere, the sphere of spirit or mind which humanizes the world. The Incarnation makes this movement a movement of divinization.

Contempt for and neglect of the material and temporal may be a religious phenomenon, but it is not a Christian attitude. To abandon society to the play of determinism is to hand it over to the Prince of this world. We must not confuse the body with what St Paul calls the flesh, nor the universe with what St John calls the world. The world and the flesh stand for those forces of evil against which the Christian must wage war in time to prepare for eternity. But matter itself is capable of salvation, as St Irenaeus reminded the "spiritual" Gnostics. Christ, by redeeming us in time, redeemed time itself, and personal salvation cannot be considered apart from the salvation of the whole human race. If at certain periods some Christians have so neglected these basic truths of their faith as to profess contempt for the world, for history and for society, that simply goes to prove the fallibility and sinfulness of their nature. Nor are we concerned because yet others have disparaged or decried political activity because they did not understand it. In fact, political action is the highest form of social action because it relates to the common good which is the condition of all other goods and hence of personal goods, and because more than any other form of activity it creates history. Politics is not an instrument of the Prince of this world, it represents the God who has caused men to live in cities. For the Christian, therefore, political activity is the highest and noblest of human occupations, second only to the religious apostolate.

To turn away from the temporal, to escape into a world of pure spirit—as if the absolutely pure life of the spirit could be compatible with human life—is to abandon the task of bringing nature and history back to God: far from supernaturalizing man, it denaturalizes him by depriving him of his social nature. This is the error of angelism, and in fact it contradicts the law of man which the Incarnation confirms and reinforces, if not the Incarnation itself. The Eternal became incarnate in time in order that eternity itself should enter into the temporal.

Spiritual and temporal

We have just raised the distinction between spiritual and temporal. It is a distinction which certain Jewish or pagan thinkers like Buddha and Socrates caught sight of, but it was left to Jesus to formulate it clearly and definitively when, holding a coin in his hands, he declared that we must render to Caesar the things that are Caesar's and to God the things that are God's. From this seemingly casual remark, from this apparently fortuitous distinction, Christians have drawn theoretical and practical conclusions which have now become part of the human consciousness itself. Indeed history has not yet exhausted its consequences, for its applications are now being made even more rigorously.

These irreversible words of Jesus are as fatal for the totalitarian neo-paganism of today as they were for the old pagan confusions: they spell freedom for persons and for society. For all his power Caesar can never claim the whole of man's allegiance, nor will God's representatives ever be able to annex Caesar's domain. In the forward movement of mankind the spiritual and the temporal connect and jostle, without ever becoming confused.

The spiritual, as the term is used in the Gospels, is to be defined by contrast not with the material or corporeal but with the temporal. The spiritual is that which does not pass away, while the temporal must of its nature pass away and die. Thus the spiritual is virtually equivalent to the eternal, and the temporal to the mortal. By spiritual we mean that which of itself relates to the person's eternal destiny, to his divine adoption and divinization. Hence it is the concern of the Church which, as the continuation of Christ, is entrusted with the task of leading the traveller to his final goal. The temporal, on the other hand, is that which does not of itself relate to this final end, that which is restricted to space and time: it is what human kind would have been had the Creator left his creatures to their own devices without giving them, in the Incarnation and Redemption, revelation and grace, that capacity for the beatific vision which belongs to them as his adopted sons. As such, water is simply a temporal creature, our good and pure sister, but when blessed it becomes spiritual, and it was to endow it with this capacity for supernaturalization that Christ sanctified it by his baptism in the Jordan. Hence to a certain degree the spiritual is to be regarded as synonymous with the supernatural, and the temporal with the natural.

The distinction between spiritual and temporal is not to be confused, as many people in our technological age seem to think, with the distinction between the moral and the technical. Technique is by definition temporal, but morality is not necessarily and intrinsically supernatural. The difference between the two distinctions is manifest in the phenomenon of culture which of itself is neither moral nor technical nor spiritual.

Nor should we make too much of this distinction, considered in isolation, if we are not to fall into what Blondel called the error of extrinsecism. We must guard against being misled by our imagination, and against using metaphorical language—by speaking, for instance, of the supernatural as "crowning" the natural. Grace perfects nature without destroying or impairing it, and to this extent we may say that the one crowns the other, but at the same time grace impregnates and fertilizes nature as rain impregnates and fertilizes the soil. Within the stream of living history, personal and human history, nature and supernature do not keep to different levels, like water and oil: they become indissolubly mingled as the one assumes, works upon and directs the other. Grace is no gratuitous and unnecessary gift for which man feels no real need, it corresponds to man's hidden aspirations, elevating him without depriving him of anything, asking nothing of him in return save only his consent to this elevation.

The kingdom of God and the kingdom of Caesar can never be coterminous: to seek to make them so is the error of theocracy or caesaropapism, a return to that state of confusion from which our Lord's words have freed us. Nevertheless, Caesar's authority comes from God, not the God of philosophers and learned men but the God of Abraham, Isaac and Jacob, the God who intervenes in history and raises man to the level of his divinity; Caesar must recognize this fact, unless he is to forswear himself. Hence if the spiritual and the temporal each have their separate sovereign and autonomous sphere of activity it seems normal that the temporal should be ordered towards the spiritual, not as means are ordered to an end nor as a part is ordered to the whole but as an end is ordered to a higher end: such a subordination is not a mere convenience, it presupposes a proper orientation of ends corresponding to their scale of importance and a proper choice of means to secure these ends. Even Caesar himself must in the end return to God.

The Incarnation does nothing to impair Caesar's dignity: on the contrary, it gives him an added dignity in so far as it sets him in pursuit of worthy ends, ends for which a man may live and die. But in its distinction between the spiritual and the temporal it gives Caesar an added reason for not proposing himself as the supreme end: it should make him recognize his limitations and prevent him from setting himself up on a pedestal. The story of Nebuchadnezzar is enough to indicate the fate which awaits those who make such claims.

A divided world

The Incarnation cannot be considered apart from the Redemption, and the well-known dispute as to whether God would have taken flesh if Adam had not sinned is of no more than speculative interest. Historically speaking, the Incarnation and the Redemption are one: the Word became flesh in order to redeem man, he accepted the conditions of temporal and bodily existence—*formam servi*—in order to release us from bondage.

This bondage was the result of the primal sin committed by Adam, the first man, who contained all human virtualities in himself just as the new Adam, Christ the Redeemer, realizes them in their fullest perfection. Original sin damaged the world and disorganized it, dislocated it, firstly by creating a duality in each person between his impaired reason and his mutinous faculties, and secondly by the consequent revolt of nature against its author and the "socialization" of sin within the human collectivity. In a divided world, persons and societies themselves become divided, not completely and intrinsically corrupt but prone to corruption, prepared even to take up the terrible apostolate of corruption.

Thus our previous remarks about the harmony which exists in spite of the inevitable tensions between persons and groups and between the common good and the particular good, need a certain amount of qualification. Harmony is in the nature of things and in the nature of man, but in fact this nature is disturbed and disordered. The effects of sin, added to the effects of contingency and human limitations, can exacerbate tensions to the point where they become intolerable, aggravating the tensions into conflicts and then turning the conflicts into endless and merciless struggles. Egoism and pride can turn the person into a mere individual, who takes himself to be the centre of the world, they can turn society into a tightly closed cell which smothers the person and regards other groups with hostility, and can make Caesar develop into a despotic and immoderate tyrant. In short, they turn man into a savage and wanton gorilla, society into what the materialist Hippolyte Taine called an amalgam of a cut-throat's den and house of ill-fame, and history into a series of blood-stained and tragic follies.

Does this mean that the doctrine of original sin leads to a radically pessimistic view of man and his work? . . . A certain pessimism may result but not the cold pessimism of certain materialists nor the scorching pessimism which pervades existentialism, for it finds expression not in disillusion and despair but in compassion and the will to gain freedom. If there is pessimism then it is a relative and active pessimism which maintains a belief in the fundamental value of human nature and regards men not as savage beasts to be broken in or tamed, but as captive brothers to be set free. Besides, it would be both illogical and anti-Christian to separate original sin from the Redemption. The effect of divine grace is to enlighten the reason and to strengthen man's liberty: the abundance of sin has been succeeded by a superabundance of grace.

Some Christians have thought fit to use the dogma of original sin as a justification for their own native pessimism, yielding, did they but know it, not only to their temperament but to original sin itself. This leads them to draw their pre-fabricated conclusions, whether it be abandoning society to the effects of original sin and to the Father of sin, or laying claim to absolute and unchecked power in order to bring men back to virtue by force. In fact the condemnation of society results in the passive acceptance of the consequences of original sin which is an intrinsically anti-Christian attitude: those who advocate authoritarian government because they claim that it will counter the effects of original sin are simply indulging in theologico-political humbug which is made even more dangerous by the fact that authorities are just as liable to original sin as their subjects, are open to even more violent temptations and hence need even more stringent control. Chesterton made original sin a justification for democracy—a paradox perhaps and yet containing more truth than the absolutism Chesterton was attacking.

The dogma of original sin has the useful effect of reminding us that we cannot simply rely on the working of social mechanisms in order to ensure liberty, progress and the common good, for these can only be won by unremitting and unceasing efforts. Secondly, we learn that in a dislocated world law cannot make justice prevail without the support of force, nor can authority secure the common good without the backing of power. Thirdly, every social equilibrium needs a system of controls, control of subordinates by superiors, and of superiors by subordinates, control of authority by the people and of the people by authority. Finally, with the distinction between the spiritual and the temporal goes an awareness that the Golden Age of the future, the earthly paradise which lies at the end of our journey, is no more than a dream: however prosperous a society may be, however perfectly organized, it is always liable to contradictions, tensions, conflicts and injustices; its prosperity and perfection are precarious achievements which the movement of life must constantly imperil. Man's duty is to make society as perfect as possible, but this perfection is always relative and limited.

The sin of the world

By the sin of the world we mean the sum total of all the sins committed since Adam's sin, the terrible avalanche of evil which progresses and grows unceasingly. The question is whether we may regard it as a collective or social sin, a sin of society as such which diminishes or does away with personal sins by absorbing them into one viscous mass. . . . This would lead us to say that in order to save men it is sufficient to reform the society. Reform must come first. To free society from sin would be to free man from sin.

Such a view cannot be maintained without certain qualifications and reservations. While the sin of the world is an overwhelmingly evident fact, this notion of collective sin demands closer examination.

Strictly speaking, there is no such thing as a collective sin, since sin presupposes responsibility and liberty which belong to persons, not to the societies composed of those persons. Collective sin is simply an accumulation of personal faults resulting from micro-decisions or macro-decisions. The concept of collective sin is obviously therefore analogical, perhaps even metaphorical, though this does not mean that it is totally meaningless or false.

In fact in certain cases it is legitimate to speak of collective sin, provided that we are clear about the precise meaning of the expression. We may say that a collective sin exists when a particular sin is so prevalent within a society that it comes to be accepted as normal behaviour and to be seen as a characteristic of that society: in Sparta homosexuality was a collective sin, while today it is immodesty and a constant incitement to eroticism. A collective sin may also be said to exist in the case of a permanent and established injustice, when one section, be it only a small minority, within a particular group finds itself sacrificed to the advantage of the rest—as with the proletariat in a nascent capitalist society. Again we may speak of a collective sin when the institutions obtaining within a society are so faulty or so unworkable that they have the effect of compelling the average man, excluding the saint, to adopt immoral practices; here we have only to think of the prohibition laws in America or the various forms of black-marketeering and cheap labour which develop in authoritarian and centralized economies. Finally, again collective sin exists when the government of a society embarks on a wrongful course of action such as an unjust war with the at least tacit complicity of most, if not all, of its members. In all these cases sin appears to be diffused throughout a collectivity.

It is clear that given man's social nature and his tendency towards imitation collective sin can sometimes attenuate or even absolve the guilt of personal sin in so far as it limits and sometimes even destroys personal freedom, particularly when it stems from incorrect collective representations.

It is no less clear that collective sins start from personal sins, be they only sins of omission, committed by the authorities or by the members of a group. As soon as the group becomes conscious of a collective sin, it ceases to have the excuse of ignorance or inadvertence: inactivity and passivity become culpable. By themselves some individuals may not be able to withstand the current of evil: their duty is to join forces in order to gain effectiveness. The ordinary man may perhaps not have the courage to put up a fight, in which case it is his duty to follow the heroes or saints who are capable of resisting. If wrongful action is due to incorrect collective representations or from faults in the framework of society, then these errors or faults must be corrected.

Original sin, sin of the world and collective sin are not to be regarded as identical. The first is a sorrowful inheritance, the second a sad fact, and the third a state of partial guilt which should never be tolerated for long. In countering collective sin the person is at the same time countering the sin of the world which he prevents from spreading further, and countering the effects of original sin. He is sharing in the work of the Redemption.

The social consequences of the Redemption

The dogma of the Redemption, too, has certain social consequences.

First, it adds enormously to the value of the human person whose redemption has cost the blood of the Man-God himself. Hence it should inspire in us a redoubled love for our fellow men, in each of whom we may see Christ incarnate, suffering and dying for us. Henceforth every man presents to us the bleeding image of Christ crucified. "Whatsoever you shall do unto him you shall do unto me" our Lord says—to me, your brother, who has redeemed you by his death.

The Redemption is also the perfect expression of that ideal of authority-service which is held up to us in the Gospels. "Let he who would be the first of all be the servant of all." The man who wields authority is the representative of Christ, and the owner of property is the steward of God, who is the one Lord and master, for authority and property are simply deposits or "talents" which he entrusts to our care so that we may turn them to the profit of our fellow men. The Christian is a man entrusted with a mission, of which he will have to render an account: he is a servant of the servants of God, and must serve not himself but others. Again, the Redemption teaches us in the sacrifice of our Lord that this service of love can and must go to the lengths of the supreme sacrifice, the surrender of life itself, which is the greatest proof of love that can be given to those one loves. Our Lord is the Good Shepherd who gives his life for his flock.

Here the dogma of the Redemption can throw light on a mystery which philosophy, because it treats it as a problem, cannot penetrate—the mystery of the total sacrifice made by the person for other persons or for the community. We may recognize the call, or even the obligation, to make this sacrifice, to the point where we forfeit our self-respect if we refuse, but at the same time we know that it brings no reward or compensation. What is the logic of sacrificing the life of the person to social organisms which only exist in order to promote the good of the person? According to their mood, men alternate between the individualistic rejection of sacrifice and a gregarious, unthinking acceptance of it. Pure philosophy has failed to penetrate this mystery, even where it asserts the existence of an after life. What is a human person without the body which sustains its spirit? The dogma of the Redemption leads straight to the dogma of the Resurrection of the body, for Christ died and rose again in order that we might die and rise again with him; they both dispel or at least throw light on our mystery. By sacrificing himself, the person is imitating Christ's sacrifice and participates in Christ's work of redemption. For him, death is not an end but a journey and at the same time a fulfilment, for on the last day he will return to life with a soul and body to enjoy the knowledge of God. He sacrifices himself, suffers, dies and rises again in union with Christ.

In the Redemption, then, human suffering finds its full meaning, whether it has its source in the person himself, in other persons or societies, in contingency, limitation or sin. The Redemption teaches us that on this earth and in our earthly conditions there can be no truly human Humanism without the Cross, the sign of contradiction, the emblem of suffering and death, the pledge of liberty. Good Friday is inconceivable without Easter, Calvary without the shattered tomb, death without Resurrection, the Cross without joy and glory. Thus the Passion comes to help us to bear our sorrows, by carrying our cross with Christ, and it unites our human hopes to a divine Hope which both embraces and transcends them. It puts us on our guard against pessimism and optimism alike by its assurance of ultimate victory in the very hour of trial or even failure.

Finally, it is the Redemption which mediates the grace that strengthens us and which, by destroying the effects of original sin, gives us the power to fight for justice and peace in the service of our fellow men. In redeeming persons the Cross of Christ redeems society and the world also.

Charity

Whether charity is to be regarded as the effect of grace or as grace itself, the two things are essentially connected. Charity is not the result of human liberty but an infused theological virtue with God as its author and object. It is obviously quite different from the purely human virtues of benevolence and beneficence and from purely human love.

We shall not dwell on the distinction between charity and almsgiving, though they have all too often been confused—to the detriment of justice and indeed of charity itself, particularly social charity. However binding it may be on every man who has superfluous wealth to dispose of, the giving of money, time, care or service is still only one among many kinds of charity. Unfortunately, it is a melancholy and significant fact that the practice of many Christians has led ordinary people to regard charity and almsgiving as synonymous.

Nor should we imagine charity to be a feigned love which one tries to show to people to whom one is not naturally and spontaneously attracted. There is, of course, an obligation of charity even towards those who are indifferent to us, even towards our adversaries and enemies: we must wish them well and do good by them. But charity is specifically different from justice in that its natural movement bears it away from the realm of obligation into the sphere of pure love.

Charity is an habitual disposition of the soul, infused and inspired by God, whereby we love God above all things, whereby we love ourselves in God, since the fact that we have been created by God makes us worthy objects of our own love, and whereby in and through God we love our neighbour as ourselves, meaning by our neighbour every man, the whole of man and all men. Love means primarily willing the good of others and acting accordingly—acting with others, not apart from them and still less in opposition to them. Charity excludes not only all egoism and self-seeking under the cloak of altruism but all clumsy interference with others: we must respect our neighbour's dignity and liberty as God respects ours. The fact that it is opposed to egoism does not mean that charity should be defined as altruistic, in the official philanthropic sense of the term; it recognizes a love of self and a love of others which is rooted in the love of God, the God who loves and redeems us all, individually and collectively. To love others in and for

God does not mean that one must not love them in and for themselves, still less does it mean that one should love them simply as instruments of one's own personal salvation; it means simply that we should always see them in relation to the God who made them and dwells within them, who is their beginning and their end. God is invisible, and so we can only prove our love for him by our love for our fellow men; they are visible, and they are at once worthy of our love and eager for it.

Charity is not primarily a matter of feeling but effective action taken for the good of others, even though this action may be prompted by feelings—emotions sometimes even stronger than conjugal or maternal love. Charity proves itself by acts, not by the fine words of high-flown sentiment. It knows no bounds since God's infinity knows no limits. If there are degrees of charity that is due not to the nature of charity itself but to the human limitations and situations which condition its effects. While, like all the virtues, it is governed by prudence, it knows no bounds in so far as God himself is not bounded, and it is precisely here that it differs from justice, which is regulated by laws of equality, proportion and reciprocity. It may go to the length of taking action which to the wise of this world appears folly, but it is the folly of love, the folly of the Cross. It differs again from justice by the gratuitousness of its gift which always exceeds what is strictly owing to or expected by others. There was no obligation on Francis of Assisi to kiss the leper's sores, nor could there be, and yet in fact he did so, thereby showing the world an example of charity in all its beauty and folly.

Charity is at once personal, interpersonal and social. Too often it has been reduced to the interpersonal. It has the whole of man for its object, and this includes man's social nature. Besides, in order to be effective it must provide the person with the social conditions which make possible his self-fulfilment. I cannot help all the men in this world who go hungry, but charity will not allow me to sleep peacefully as long as I know that my fellow men are hungry, without having done anything to feed them. Charity impels me to render immediate help to those who suffer from injustice in body or spirit, and yet it does not rest content with such provisional palliatives: the primary charity towards the victims of injustice is to see that they obtain justice. How can one abandon men to injustice and then claim to love them? To the latter it would seem hypocrisy, and for oneself it would be self-delusion. Charity also acts as an incentive to justice, particularly to distributive, social and international justice, and it fosters a restless desire for improvement, a longing for perfection. It can never rest content. In its social rôle, therefore, it is not confined to being a mere ancillary or complement of justice, as too often has been imagined. It completes justice, certainly, but at the same time it outstrips, precedes and establishes it.

It has been said that charity is the cement of society. The metaphor is a rather crude one: charity should be thought of rather as the blood or the soul of society, that which animates it or gives it life. It is the basis of society, founding it on God who is its author and object, establishing and fostering communal love, civic friendship and social goodwill. There is no social order without justice, and there is no justice without charity. Charity creates unity among men by that love whereby the Father and the Son are one. It establishes the reign of peace in and through Christ, our Father.

Though in non-Christian civilizations we may find justice, goodwill, beneficence, fellowship, equity and piety—the natural social virtues of man—charity is absent. That does not mean that charity has always held absolute sway among Christian peoples but it has pervaded Christian society: it is the cause of the social progress it has initiated and of the divine discontent which urges them forward and prevents them from resting content with whatever measure of justice they may at any time have obtained.

The Mystical Body of the Church

Grace and charity, which together constitute the divine life of man, unite the Mystical Body of which Christ is the Head and we the members, each with his own function.

The Mystical Body is the full and perfect realization of the human ideal of the community, which it nevertheless transcends. It fulfils the deepest aspirations of human nature while at the same time it gives man something that exceeds his wildest dreams, an unimagined and unprecedented superfluity: it is rooted in nature and in a supernature which is not opposed to nature since both come from God. It demands from man a complete commitment of body and soul, for time and eternity, operating from within him solely by the power of love, without pressure or constraint. It finds its embodiment in the most perfect of all fellowships, the communion of saints, in which all merits are shared, everything being in common between Head and members and between the members themselves—a fellowship which persists beyond time into eternity. It is the source of joys which we shall only fully discover in the heavenly Jerusalem but of which some men are granted a foretaste on this earth in an experimental union with God through and in Christ: *per ipsum, cum ipso, et in ipso.*

In the Mystical Body man may find what he looks for in earthly communities without ever fully attaining—the harmonious fulfilment of his personal and social being; the perfect realization of his vocation to love God within his particular situation and to be united to God while remaining a human person; diverse members and diverse vocations united in one body; perfect liberty existing in a perfect community, the communion of saints; a belonging, a membership, a full and unqualified participation—in short, self-realization in communion with others.

The Mystical Body, therefore, is the ideal and exemplar of the Community towards which all human societies should strive.

This community, which is coextensive with history, ever

suffering and ever advancing until it reaches the fullness of the Eighth Day, takes partial shape in the visible Church here on earth. The Church, however, necessarily involves contingency, limitation and weaknesses: some of those who regard themselves as inside it are really outside and some of those who regard themselves as outside it are really inside. For the sociologist who studies it from without, and *a fortiori* for the faithful Christian who looks at it from within, the Church is a community, a community which demands a total commitment, a community based on natural religion and on supernatural revelation, a community which shares the same destiny, the same sufferings and joys. It is not an accident that the various groups which it incorporates go by the name of communities.

The Christian fraternity

Within the Mystical Body men are brothers. They are brothers who share the same Father, their heavenly Father, whose sons they are by creation and again by divine adoption. One of the major inconsistencies of our time has been the attempt to maintain the concept and the reality of brotherhood without relation to the universal and transcendent Fatherhood.

Men are brothers, again, in the brotherhood of the God-Man, the first-born among men, through whom we have received the Holy Spirit who makes it possible for us to call God our father and to respond to the grace of divine adoption.

They are brothers too as sons of the Virgin Mary, the new Eve, mother of the living, who by her *Fiat* consented to receive Christ's gift to mankind.

They are brothers by reason of the one charity which unites them and inspires them to brotherly action, brothers in the communion of saints which ceaselessly maintains between them a mysterious current of fraternal love.

Theirs is a brotherhood which knows no limits, making no discrimination between persons, races, classes, nations or civilizations.

The visible sign of this brotherhood is the Eucharist which is a memorial of the death of the Saviour, commemorating the sacrifices of the Brother of all men who has given his life for his brethren, and a family in which the brethren share the bread and wine which are the flesh and blood of their brother. The Eucharist is also Communion, the sacrament of unity in which the fraternal community finds its meaning and foundation.

It follows that the Christian ideal of society must be one of brotherhood; brotherhood within the group and between the groups themselves, until the whole world shall be one brotherhood united in the love of the Father.

Towards the City of God

History is the meeting-place, the point of contact between the Mystical Body of Christ, the visible Church and the world. But real history, the history which lies behind appearances, is the history of the City of God which is built by the succeeding generations of men. We may recall St Augustine's allegory: "Two loves have built two cities. . . ." In fact there is only one love which is truly constructive, and that is charity. Whatever is built on the love of self, on the religion of the individual or group, is doomed to break up and decay.

Little by little the City of God is built as the Mystical Body slowly grows to its full size—its pleroma—in the building yard of history. It is a work of ceaseless construction, demolition and reconstruction. It is a process which goes unseen by men, unmentioned by historians and even by Christians perceived only with the eyes of faith. But the City is there, present, living, slowly being built up, stone by stone, upon the deeds of persons and the persons themselves. It is charity which brings the bricklayers, charity which mixes the cement and climbs the scaffolding.

That which we can see now only in a glass darkly we shall see one day in the light of God, illuminating our sight and the sight of our brethren from within. That will be the Day of

Judgement, the day when Christ, the Sun of Justice, the Prince of Peace, will come to judge the living and the dead, not just to judge individual persons but, in virtue of man's social nature, to judge all mankind and all history. All things will be summed up in him.

Then the heaven and earth of time will give place to a new earth and a new heaven, to the City of God, the heavenly Jerusalem, blessed vision of eternal peace, which will be none other than the Mystical Body now grown to its full stature of maturity by its passage from time to eternity and from grace to glory.

Renewed in Christ, man will find in him everything for which his personal nature and his social nature yearn: the reconciliation of personal separateness with unity and love; eternal peace established in eternal justice; a transparency which makes all persons open to each other in the uncreated Light; an absolute system of graded functions untouched by contingency; full participation coexisting with full liberty; one community living in eternal joy.

We must not think, however, that our earthly cities and their achievements will be obliterated in the eternal city.

> "Happy the men who die for the cities of earth,
> For of these is made the City of God."

Charles Péguy was no theologian, but his insight here is profound. Jerusalem is built of living stones, of persons, and these persons who there achieve their eternal fulfilment are in part what their societies and communities, their earthly cities, have made them. Thus by a mysterious transmutation the Cities of time will subsist in eternity: the persons who find their fulfilment in eternity were once their citizens. *Urbs Jerusalem beata. . . .* : Jerusalem, the holy and blessed city of which the Dedication hymn sings, is both an earthly and a heavenly city.

On this note, with this vision, we end our essay in social theology which has followed the order of the *Credo*, ending with the final *Et vitam venturi saeculi. Amen.* And so our essay in social anthropology ends with a theological vista, the vista which reveals the final stage of man's journey. Society is only fully human where man can transcend it.

SELECT BIBLIOGRAPHY

In this series: Bovis, André de, S.J.: *The Church: Christ's Mystery and Sacrament*; Le Trocquer, René: *What is Man?*; Rétif, Louis and André: *The Mission of the Church in the World.*

Bergson, Henri: *The Two Sources of Morality and Religion*, New York, Henry Holt, 1935.

Daniélou, J., S.J.: *The Salvation of the Nations*, London and New York, Sheed and Ward, 1949.

Hawkins, D. B. J.: *Man and Morals*, London and New York, Sheed and Ward, 1960.

Hughes, Philip: *The Popes' New Order: A Systematic Study of the Social Encyclicals and Addresses from Leo XIII to Pius XII*, London, Burns and Oates, 1943.

Lubac, Henri de, S.J.: *Catholicism, A Study of Dogma in Relation to the Corporate Destiny of Mankind*, translated by Lancelot C. Sheppard, London, Burns and Oates, and New York, Sheed and Ward, 1950.

Maritain, Jacques: *The Person and the Common Good*, London, Bles, and New York, Scribner, 1952.

Mounier, Emmanuel: *Be not Afraid*, London, Rockliff, and New York, Harper, 1954; *Character of Man*, New York, Harper, 1957.

Mouroux, J.: *The Meaning of Man*, London and New York, Sheed and Ward, 1950.

Schmidt, W.: *The Origin and Growth of Religion*, London, Methuen, 1931; *High Gods in North America*, Oxford, Clarendon Press, 1933.

Seligman, E. R. A., and Johnson, A. (Editors): *Encyclopedia of Social Sciences*, 15 volumes, New York, Macmillan, 1950–6.

Teilhard de Chardin, P., S.J.: *The Phenomenon of Man*, London, Collins, and New York, Harper, 1959; *The Milieu Divin*, London, Collins, and New York, Harper, 1961.

The Twentieth Century Encyclopedia of Catholicism

The number of each volume indicates its place in the over-all series and not the order of publication.

PART ONE: KNOWLEDGE AND FAITH

1. What Does Man Know?
2. Is Theology a Science?
3. The Meaning of Tradition
4. The Foundations of Faith
5. Do Dogmas Change?
6. What is Faith?
7. God's Word to Man
8. Myth or Mystery?
9. What is a Miracle?
10. Is There a Christian Philosophy?
11. The Origins of Christian Philosophy
12. Medieval Christian Philosophy
13. The Basis of Belief
14. Christianity and Science
15. The God of Reason

PART TWO: THE BASIC TRUTHS

16. The Worship of God
17. What is the Trinity?
18. The Holy Spirit
19. The Creation
20. The Problem of Evil
21. Who is the Devil?
22. Freedom and Providence
23. The Theology of Grace
24. What is the Incarnation?
25. What is Redemption?
26. The Communion of Saints
27. Faith, Hope and Charity
28. Life After Death

PART THREE: THE NATURE OF MAN
29. The Origins of Man
30. Evolution
31. What is Man?
32. What is Life?
33. Personal Responsibility
34. Man in His Environment
35. Man and Metaphysics
36. Psychical Phenomena
PART FOUR: THE MEANS OF REDEMPTION
37. Prayer
38. The Nature of Mysticism
39. Spiritual Writers of the Early Church
40. Spiritual Writers of the Middle Ages
41. Post-Reformation Spirituality
42. Spiritual Writers in the Modern Period
43. True and False Possession
44. Mary the Mother of God
45. The Devotion to Our Lady
46. What is a Saint?
47. What is an Angel?
PART FIVE: THE LIFE OF FAITH
48. What is the Church?
49. What is a Sacrament?
50. Christian Initiation
51. Penance and Absolution
52. What is the Eucharist?
53. What is a Priest?
54. Christian Marriage
55. Death and the Christian
56. What is Christian Life?
57. The Enigma of the Stigmata
58. Christian Ethics
59. Christianity and Money
PART SIX: THE WORD OF GOD
60. What is the Bible?
61. The Promised Land
62. Biblical Archaeology
63. Biblical Criticism
64. God's People in the Bible
65. The Religion of Israel
66. The Prophets
67. The Sources for the Life of Christ
68. The Life of Our Lord
69. What is the Gospel?
70. St. Paul and His Message

71. What the Old Testament Does Not Tell Us
72. The New Testament Apocrypha
73. Judaism

PART SEVEN: THE HISTORY OF THE CHURCH

74. Christian Beginnings
75. The Dawn of the Middle Ages
76. The Early Middle Ages
77. The Later Middle Ages
78. The Revolt Against the Church
79. The Church in the Eighteenth Century

PART EIGHT: THE ORGANIZATION OF THE CHURCH

80. What is Canon Law?
81. The Papacy
82. The Ecumenical Councils
83. What is a Bishop?
84. The Organization of the Church
85. Religious Orders of Men
86. Religious Orders of Women
87. Secular Institutes
88. The Catholic Spirit

PART NINE: THE CHURCH AND THE MODERN WORLD

89. Church and State
90. Christianity and Economics
91. Atheism
92. A History of Catholicism in the English-speaking World
93. Psychiatry and the Christian
94. Christianity and the Machine Age
95. The Christian and World Integration
96. Christianity and Communism
97. Christianity and Colonialism
98. Holiness in Action
99. History of the Missions
100. Missions in the World Today
101. The Contribution of German Catholicism
102. The Church's Mission in the World
103. The Church and Sex
104. Law and Morals
105. Christian Charity in Action
106. International Morality
107. Why We Believe

PART TEN: THE WORSHIP OF THE CHURCH

108. The Spirit of Worship
109. The Liturgical Books
110. History of the Mass
111. The Mass in the West
112. Eastern Liturgies

113. The Christian Calendar
114. Vestments and Church Furniture
115. The Liturgical Movement

PART ELEVEN: CATHOLICISM AND LITERATURE

116. Sacred Languages
117. Christian Literature Today
118. Christian Poetry
119. Modern Christian Literature

PART TWELVE: CATHOLICISM AND THE ARTS

120. The Christian Meaning of Art
121. Early Christian Art
122. Church Building
123. Christian Art in the 19th and 20th Centuries
124. Christian Theatre
125. Christian Music
126. Motion Pictures, Radio and Television

PART THIRTEEN: CATHOLICISM AND SCIENCE

127. Embryo and Anima
128. Nuclear Physics in Peace and War
129. Medicine and Morals
130. Science and Religion
131. Cybernetics
132. World Poverty and the Christian
133. Towards A Theology of Science
134. To be assigned

PART FOURTEEN: OUTSIDE THE CHURCH

135. The Spirit of Eastern Orthodoxy
136. Heresies and Heretics
137. Protestantism
138. Christian Unity
139. Christian Sects

PART FIFTEEN: NON-CHRISTIAN BELIEFS

140. Primitive and Prehistoric Religions
141. Religions of the Ancient East
142. Greek and Roman Religion
143. Mohammedanism
144. Hinduism
145. Buddhism
146. Mystery Cults
147. Superstition
148. Christianity and Other Religions

PART SIXTEEN: GENERAL AND SUPPLEMENTARY VOLUMES

149. Why I am a Christian
150. Index

All titles are subject to change.